The WoodenBoat Series

FRAME, STEM & KEEL REPAIR

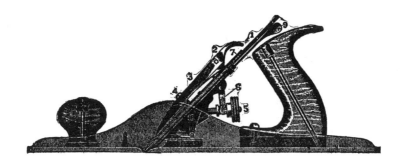

Series Editor, Peter H. Spectre

Copyright ©1996
by WoodenBoat Publications, Inc.
ISBN 0-937822-42-6

Cover and text design by Richard Gorski
Cover photograph by Benjamin Mendlowitz

Published by WoodenBoat Publications
P.O. Box 78, Naskeag Road
Brooklin, Maine 04616-0078

Introduction

Many years ago a lightbulb blew out in the stairwell of the first house I ever owned, an old Victorian. No problem, I said to myself.

I pulled the fuse, got out a ladder, climbed up with a new lightbulb, and unscrewed the old one. The socket, about 75 years old, crumbled in my hands. No problem, I said to myself.

I went to the hardware store, bought a new socket, took it home, climbed the ladder, and unscrewed the light fixture from the ceiling. The lamp cord, about 75 years old, crumbled in my hands. No problem, I said to myself.

I went to the hardware store, bought a new length of lamp cord, took it home, climbed the ladder, and unwound the electrician's tape from the splice between the old lamp cord and the house wiring. The insulation crumbled in my hands. Big problem, I said to myself.

The upshot was that I had to rewire the entire circuit. A simple ten-minute job — replace a lightbulb — became a major electrical restoration lasting several days. In the process, I discovered a few structural matters that needed attention....

I have been thinking about that experience while assembling the material for this book. Old houses, old boats. The problems are the same. Just when you think you have a repair in hand, you pull the mess aside and discover something underneath that's just as bad, or worse.

Dig down far enough in a wooden boat, and you come to the heart of the matter, the foundation of everything else — the frames, the keel, and the stem. They are analogous to the sill, joists, rafters, and framing of a house. If they have integrity, the structure has integrity. If they don't, they must be fixed or the structure will not survive.

I realize that is easier said than done, but it can be done, and the proof of that can be seen in this book. Look, for example, at what Keith Quarrier was able to do with a tired old St. Lawrence skiff. Look at how Steve Ballentine pulled the keel and centerboard trunk from a Buzzards Bay 15 built in 1914 and replaced them with new members. Look at how Benjamin River Marine put in a new stem for *Whippet*, and Brooklin Boat Yard did the same thing for the powerboat *Kittiwake II*. Look at Ed McClave's new frames for *Spartan* and Peter Boudreau's new timbers for *Gazela*. Look at the steam box rigs patched together by amateurs who wouldn't allow anything to get in the way of their desire to get the job done.

The fact is that if a boat is worth saving, it can be saved. People — both amateurs and professionals — do it all the time. If they don't know how to do it, they find someone who does.

There are times, however, when you can't find someone to advise you on how to do it. That's when this book comes into its own. While it is not the last word on frame, stem, and keel repair, it contains enough collective wisdom to answer most boat repairers' questions and then some.

As in all works that collect together advice and information from many sources, there are a few disagreements among authors and some repetition, but that is to be expected in a field that has so few hard-and-fast rules. Most people who repair wooden boats have gained their knowledge from experience, and, as most similar experiences are nevertheless somewhat different from each other, the advice they induce is sometimes slightly different. The reader's job, then, is to sort through the advice, determine how it may or may not apply to the situation at hand, and take it from there.

There are any number of people who, when asked, will tell you how to steam-bend the stem of a small open rowing boat. They may never have steamed such a stem themselves, but they met someone once who knew someone who heard that someone else had done it 20 years ago.... Here, in this book, we have a chapter from a professional boatbuilder who steamed 11 stems for Rangeley boats at the Mystic Seaport boatbuilding shop. His experience is considerable; his advice is to be believed.

I don't know about you, but when I undertake a project that is new to me, I leave no stone unturned in researching the subject. The first time I steamed a frame, for example, I talked to all the boatbuilders I knew and read all the material I could find. The reading material, as you would expect, was spread out all over the place. Here, we have it collected together, and the beauty is that it is based on practice, not theory.

—Peter H. Spectre
Camden, Maine

About the Authors

J. MURRAY ABERCROMBIE is a professional boatbuilder of nearly 25 years' standing; he lives in Quathiaski Cove, British Columbia.

CLIFTON ANDREWS is one of the earliest contributors to *WoodenBoat* magazine.

WILLITS ANSEL of Georgetown, Maine, has worked as a ship carpenter at Mystic Seaport Museum and served as director of the Apprenticeshop at the Maine Maritime Museum; he has written several monographs and articles on wooden boat building.

WALTER BARON is a professional boatbuilder in Wellfleet, Massachusetts.

CHRISTIAN BLUMEL is a boatbuilder in Bremen, Germany.

PETER BOUDREAU of Annapolis, Maryland, worked on the construction of the *Pride of Baltimore* and was the master builder of *Pride of Baltimore II* and the *Lady Maryland*.

MAYNARD BRAY, former shipyard supervisor at Mystic Seaport Museum, is the author of numerous articles and books on wooden boat building and repair. A contributing editor of *WoodenBoat* magazine, he lives in Brooklin, Maine.

ARCH DAVIS, originally from New Zealand, lives in Maine, where he designs, builds, and writes about boats.

MICHAEL DZIUBINSKI has a degree in architecture and is also a graduate of the Rockport Apprenticeshop. He has worked as a boatbuilder in Wisconsin, France, and Vermont.

R.L. ELTON of Orchard Lake, Michigan, has restored a 1940 GarWood runabout.

J.W. ENGLAND, JR., of Burgess, Virginia, has been building traditional wooden boats since his retirement in 1977.

KEN AND MO FRASER of Galiano Island, British Columbia, milled their own lumber, built their own boat, and cruised the Pacific Ocean for two and a half years.

RONALD HEARON, an officer of the South Jersey Chapter of the Traditional Small Craft Association, builds and repairs wooden boats.

ULF HENRIKSON, a former wooden boat restorer, is a retailer of screws, nails, and other fasteners for woodworking in Stockholm, Sweden.

RICH HILSINGER is the director of WoodenBoat School in Brooklin, Maine.

RICHARD JAGELS, the long-time author of the "Wood Technology" column in *WoodenBoat* magazine, is a professor in the Department of Forestry at the University of Maine in Orono, Maine.

DANIEL MACNAUGHTON is a part owner and operations manager of Eastport Boat Yard & Supply of Eastport, Maine. He served as associate editor of *WoodenBoat* magazine for many years.

SAMUEL F. MANNING of Camden, Maine, is an artist, writer, and illustrator specializing in traditional maritime subjects. He has illustrated many articles and books, including John Gardner's *Dory Book* and Bud McIntosh's *How to Build a Wooden Boat*.

STEVE MAYES of Maple Ridge, British Columbia, is retired and is building a Nereia, an L. Francis Herreshoff design, for his own use.

EDWARD F. MCCLAVE of Noank, Connecticut, has been building and restoring wooden boats for more than two decades. A member of the Society of Naval Architects and Marine Engineers, he has contributed many articles to *WoodenBoat* magazine.

JOSEPH P. PERRY, following retirement, has taken up serious boatbuilding as an avocation; he lives in Worcester, Massachusetts.

KEITH QUARRIER, a teacher of woodworking and boatbuilding for 15 years, builds and repairs St. Lawrence skiffs and other small craft in Alstead, New Hampshire.

TERRY RIDINGS is an amateur boat restorer in Sidney, British Columbia.

D.W. ROLSTONE builds and repairs boats, with a specialty in interior joinery, in Dyfed, Wales.

C. GREG RÖSSEL, a frequent contributor to *WoodenBoat* magazine and an instructor at WoodenBoat School, builds and repairs boats in Troy, Maine.

D.W. STONER, a wooden boat enthusiast, lives in York, Pennsylvania.

SIMON WATTS, based in San Francisco, California, is a longtime teacher of boatbuilding classes around the country and a founder of the Arques School of Traditional Boatbuilding in Sausalito, California.

RALPH C. WERNETT of Warwick, Rhode Island, is an amateur repairer and restorer of wooden boats.

JON WILSON of Brooklin, Maine, is the founder and editor-in-chief of *WoodenBoat* magazine.

JAMES WOODWARD is one of the earliest contributors to *WoodenBoat* magazine.

Table of Contents

Why Bent Frames Break, and How to Fix Them

by Edward F. McClave with drawings by Kathy Bray

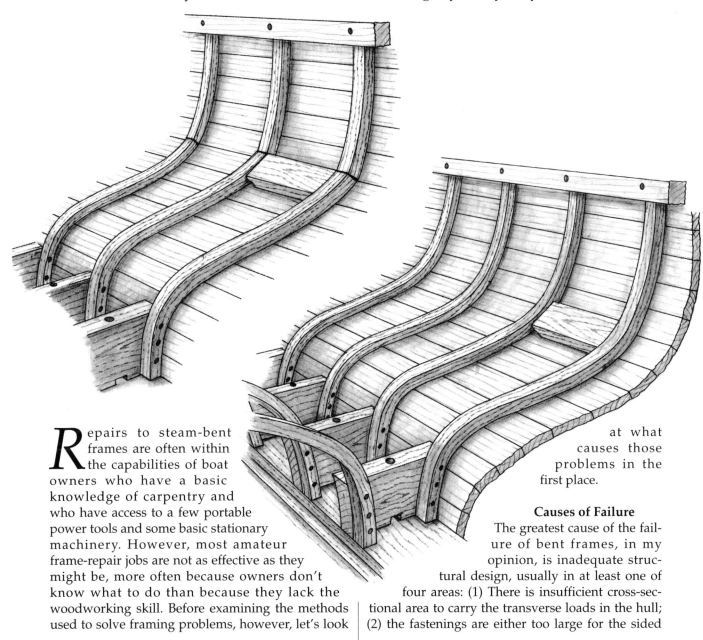

Repairs to steam-bent frames are often within the capabilities of boat owners who have a basic knowledge of carpentry and who have access to a few portable power tools and some basic stationary machinery. However, most amateur frame-repair jobs are not as effective as they might be, more often because owners don't know what to do than because they lack the woodworking skill. Before examining the methods used to solve framing problems, however, let's look at what causes those problems in the first place.

Causes of Failure

The greatest cause of the failure of bent frames, in my opinion, is inadequate structural design, usually in at least one of four areas: (1) There is insufficient cross-sectional area to carry the transverse loads in the hull; (2) the fastenings are either too large for the sided

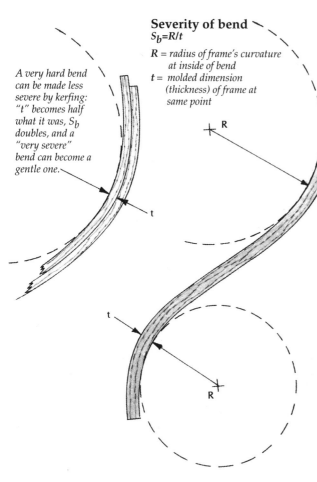

Severity of bend
$$S_b = R/t$$

R = radius of frame's curvature at inside of bend

t = molded dimension (thickness) of frame at same point

A very hard bend can be made less severe by kerfing: "t" becomes half what it was, S_b doubles, and a "very severe" bend can become a gentle one.

Gentle Bend: S_b = 20 (long-lived frame)
Moderate Bend: S_b = 14–20 (some breakage)
Hard Bend: S_b = 10–14 (premature breakage)
Very Hard Bend: S_b = 10 (nearly broken by bending)

Frames fail most often in tension

Tensile cracks are fairly ragged and start at the convex face, usually at a fastening. A frame breaks when a crack extends to the concave face of the frame and the wood shears off between fastening holes.

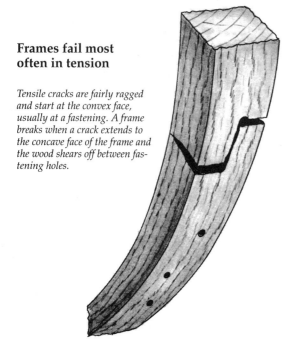

dimension of the frame or too close to the edge of the frame; (3) the frames have been weakened because they were bent to a curve that was too severe; (4) internal longitudinal members, such as bilge stringers and sheer clamps, are improperly designed.

Frames also weaken and break sometimes as the result of poor repair practices, particularly because of improper refastening. They can decay as well from contact with fresh water, rusting iron or steel fastenings, steel strapping or chainplates, or dezincifying brass or Tobin bronze strapping. Frames of red oak, in particular, are prone to all types of decay, considerably more so than frames of white oak. Very old frames can fail just from slow decomposition due to age. Sailing stresses, engine loads, collisions, groundings, or other external conditions beyond the boat's designed capabilities also cause frame failure, usually when they are combined with other weaknesses.

Tensile Cracks and Breaks

Tensile cracks and breaks are the most common frame problem. The cracks usually start at the convex face and extend inward to about the middle of the frame, although sometimes the frame is completely severed. When the cracks are small and numerous, and occur in more than just one frame, the problem is caused either by excessive severity of bend or by fastenings being placed too close to the edge of the frame. The same problem often occurs in the reverse curve near frame heels, this time on the face of the frame toward the inside of the boat. In this situation, the frame may split rather than crack. Excessive severity of bend is usually the culprit here, although improper placement of floor-to-frame fastenings can encourage failure of frame heels as well.

Severity of bend is the ratio of the radius of curvature of the bend at any given point to the molded dimension of the frame at the same point (the radius is measured to the inside of the curve, or the concave face, of the frame). When the severity of bend is between 20 and 14, the frame is slightly weakened in its ability to carry tension; unless they are subjected to an excessive or concentrated stress, most gently bent frames perform satisfactorily. When the severity is 14 to 12, the likelihood of frame breakage increases considerably, all other things being equal; when the severity is 12 to 10, you can be assured of considerable premature breakage. When the severity is less than 10, the frame will be nearly broken by the act of bending it, and the added stress from service aboard a boat will surely cause it to fail. To put this another way: because the frame didn't break when it was steambent is not a guarantee that it will not fail later. If the severity of curvature is less than 14 for a solid frame, you can ease the severity by slitting or kerfing the frame to create two layers before bending.

Cracks due to severe bending almost always occur at fastenings, and if the fastenings are not selected or put in properly, the chance of frame breakage is much higher. The center of any fastening hole in a frame bent more severely than 20 should be no closer to the edge of the frame than two-and-a-half times the shank diameter of the fastening. This means that if the fastenings are not staggered, the sided dimensions of the frame must be at least five times the fastening diameter, and, if staggered, five times plus the stagger. For bends with severity less than 14, the distance from fastening hole to frame edge should be approximately three times the fastening diameter.

When multiple cracking occurs, the frame often lasts for many years without further damage or serious loss of shape, especially when the hull is double planked. In single-planked hulls, these cracks usually develop slowly into more serious fractures, accompanied by hard spots in the frame's curvature.

Complete breaks in frames may be caused by tensile loads beyond the capability of the frames to handle, or to normal loads on a frame already cracked and weakened. These breaks tend to cluster

Relationship of frames and fastenings

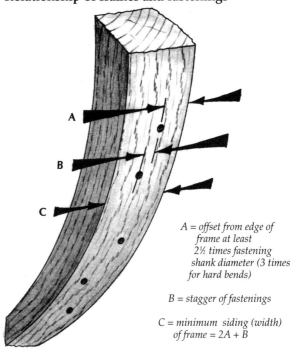

A = offset from edge of frame at least 2½ times fastening shank diameter (3 times for hard bends)

B = stagger of fastenings

C = minimum siding (width) of frame = 2A + B

in adjacent frames. Here's a possible sequence of events:

One frame breaks, and the loads it once carried fall on its neighboring frames, perhaps causing them to fail as well. The hull develops a hard spot at the break and starts to leak, since the frames are no longer able to resist the compression on the caulking seam. In an attempt to correct the problem, an owner may recaulk the area, putting even more stress on the neighboring frames, and may even refasten the planks, further weakening the frames until they break. In this fashion, the problem continues to spread along the seam and the boat progressively loses its shape.

Tensile breaks are a particular characteristic of single-planked mahogany hulls, because mahogany has a high compressive strength and thus swells powerfully when it takes on moisture after the boat is launched. This problem is often accentuated by the moisture content of the mahogany planking stock. Mahogany used for planking is commonly much drier than other planking materials, and thus

Finding the radius of curvature

$$R = \frac{(h)^2 + (C/2)^2}{2h}$$

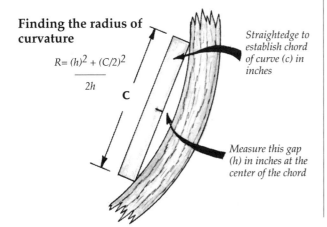

Straightedge to establish chord of curve (c) in inches

Measure this gap (h) in inches at the center of the chord

Let the gap be the guide in estimating bend severity. Some examples:

Frame Molding	Gap (h) Over 12" Chord Length (c)		
	Gentle Bend	*Moderate Bend*	*Very Hard Bend*
¾"	1 ¼"	1 ⅞"	3"
1"	⅞"	1 ⅜"	2"
1 ¼"	¾"	1"	1 ½"
1 ½"	⅝"	⅞"	1 ¼"

Frame broken by bilge stringer

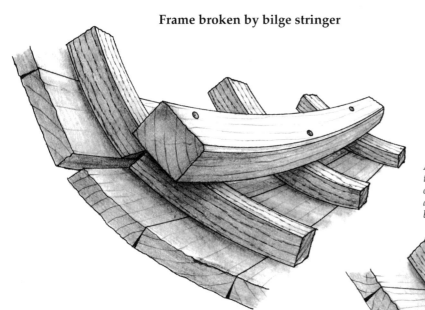

A proper bilge stringer

A proper bilge stringer should be no more than 15 percent thicker than the planking and at least 4 times wider than its own thickness. Its underside should be crowned for good fit against the frames. Fastenings should be screws rather than bolts where practical.

it swells more when the boat is launched. If a mahogany hull is even slightly overcaulked, or if the frames are not of sufficient cross section, you're in for problems that generally won't occur in hulls planked with softer, more forgiving wood. The frame spacing and scantlings for mahogany-planked hulls should not be less than those given in Nevins's scantling rule, and particular care must be taken to avoid severe bends and improper fastenings.

Effects of Bilge Stringers

The concentrated stresses in bent frames from contact with stringers are responsible for a great many broken frames and deformed boats. In my opinion, bilge stringers — a vestigial holdover from the days of sailing ships and large schooners — can be eliminated in moderate-sized yachts, at least in many cases. Stringers are often too stiff and bear on a very small area of the frame. When the rest of the boat flexes, the part of the frame under the stringer is held rigid and is likely to break. Frames are further weakened at this critical intersection by the large through-bolts that are frequently used to fasten stringers in place.

Where bilge stringers are used, they should never be more than about 15 percent thicker than the planking and under no circumstances thicker than the molded dimension of the frame. These rules apply to seat risers in small boats, as well. In addition, stringers should never be narrower than three times their thickness. They should be carefully rounded on the contact face so that they fit well

against each frame over their full width. If bilge stringers are through-fastened, the fastenings should follow the guidelines for plank fastenings set down earlier. It is better to screw-fasten bilge stringers than to use large through-bolts (thus avoiding another fastening through the "tension" part of the frame), although bolts may be necessary in large boats.

Split Frame Heels

Improper size and placement of floor-to-frame bolts can cause split and broken frame heels. As a general rule, the diameter of floor-to-frame fastenings should not exceed one-fifth the molded dimension of the frame, and whenever possible these fastenings should be kept on center or a little toward the compression side (the side toward the concave face) of the frame. Floorboard support beams should be notched over the frames and bear against them, rather than depend entirely upon their fastenings for support.

Engine beds can cause similar problems, as can sheer clamps, which often break frames up high and aft where only a corner of the clamp contacts the frame.

Shear Failures

Clean, square breaks across a frame in line with a plank seam generally indicate shear failure. Often caused by external damage, such breaks are frequently seen just above the tops of the floor timbers in boats that have run aground fast and hard. In this situation, the keel and lower part of the boat come to an abrupt stop, while the part of the boat above the floor timbers tries to keep going; when the planks slide by each other a bit, the frames can snap off.

Shear failure is also caused by the flexing of the hull under twisting loads. In this case, the failures are usually found within a diagonal swath of hull between the chainplates and the center of the ballast, where the torsional loads are the greatest. A loosely caulked single-planked hull is most prone to this problem; it rarely occurs in double-planked or diagonally strapped hulls.

Strategies of Frame Repair

The first step in frame repair is to find out in detail just what is wrong and how the problem developed, so the repair can be made without a recurrence. Whether the boat is damaged by collision, weakened by previous repairs, or simply old and tired, a complete and detailed survey of the entire boat — not just the frames — is in order. Since the ultimate decision about how to fix the frames depends as much on the overall condition of the rest of the boat as it does on the frames themselves, be thorough. Professional help is probably more valuable to you now than during any other stage of the job, and unless you are intimately familiar with wooden boat construction, ask an experienced boat carpenter or a good surveyor to go over the boat with you.

Hard spots and open seams at the turn of the bilge on the outside of the hull are a sure sign of frame problems on the inside. Check the way the boat is supported. If the poppets are pushing up into the hull, there may be problems behind them. Find out what the fastenings are (nails, screws, or rivets), what material, what size (if screws), and whether they can still be withdrawn. Look for evidence of refastening. This information will help you decide what to do and may also provide clues as to why the frames broke.

Go over the inside of the hull with a fine-tooth comb. If there's much joinerwork or ceiling, remove all that you can and use every means available to inspect every possible inch of every possible frame.

Use mirrors, flashlights, fiber optics, whatever. The more you see now, the fewer surprises you'll have later. Look especially for unfair spots on the inside of the planking. Hard spots may have been faired off on the outside, but they can't be hidden on the inside. Open seams or unfairness on the inside usually indicate broken frames. Cracks in frames may be difficult to see in bad lighting, or if they are covered by paint. Look for cracks along the side of the frame right where it contacts the plank. These cracks are almost always in line with the fastenings, which are, of course, near the edges of the planks (edges of the outer planking in double-planked hulls).

Check the heels of the frames for cracks, splits, and decay. Look at the floor-to-frame fastenings, and, while you're at it, check the floor timbers themselves for splits (usually at the floor-to-frame bolts), decay, or crushed wood under the keelbolt nuts. Floor timbers should be considered a part of the frames — a link in the chain, so to speak. It doesn't make sense to put the frames in tiptop condition if the floors are not in equally good shape.

Next, take a careful look under the bilge stringer for cracked frames. Check the frame heads for decay; also check any place where the frames touch metal, such as the chainplates or diagonal strapping. Be sure to check under the sheer clamp aft

Proper location of floor-to-frame fastenings

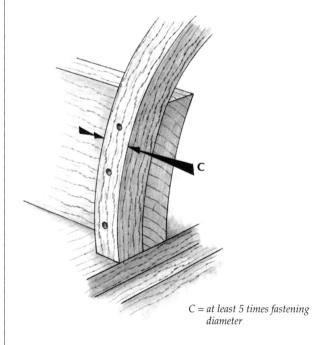

C = at least 5 times fastening diameter

(where the bend is usually severe) for cracked frames.

Are there sister frames? If so, are they doing their job or are they too short or have they broken like the originals? Measure the size of the fastenings (if you are able to extract any) and compare them to the frame scantlings. Look to see how they were staggered and how close to the edge of the frames they came in places where the frames have broken. Check the radius of curvature of the concave face of broken or cracked frames, compare this to the molded dimension of the frames, and evaluate the severity of the bend. Measure the dimensions, length, and taper of the frames to get an idea of what materials you'll need. Think about what joinerwork will have to be removed for access.

Keep going with this inspection and examine the rest of the boat in the same way. Look at the backbone: the keel, horn timber, stem, deadwood, and transom; then at the planking; and finally at the deck. When you have digested all this information (you wrote all of it down, didn't you?), decide what to do about the boat's frame problems.

It doesn't make sense to put one part of the boat in better condition than you plan to put the rest of the boat in, and it's really foolish to cover over problem areas with new work. Don't bother working on frames and floor timbers if the keel or horn timber is rotten; don't waste time putting on a lot of new planks if the frames behind them are bad; and certainly don't put a new deck on a boat if everything from the deck down isn't in good shape. Thus, the logical sequence of repairs, whether you're doing the work all at once or doing one item a year, is the keel and backbone first, then the floor timbers and frames, the planking next, then the deck, and, finally, the joinerwork.

Frame repairs fall into two broad categories: out-and-out replacement, and the installation of sister frames. Replacing damaged frames with new ones, if done properly, can restore a boat to its original strength and shape without adding extra weight. Reframing also preserves or increases a boat's resale value, although the process can be involved and expensive in terms of labor.

By contrast, sister framing — placing a new frame next to an existing cracked or broken frame — is a stabilization measure that keeps a boat from falling apart any further. If the boat's shape has been lost because of frame breakage, it is unlikely that it can be restored to normal by this method of repair. Sister framing adds weight and requires the drilling of more holes in the planking, tending to weaken it. Sister frames are rarely able to carry transverse loads as well as the original frames. However, sistering is usually a lot cheaper than frame replacement and can be accomplished more quickly and with less disturbance to the rest of the boat.

Replacing frames in a small, open boat is often just as easy as sistering, whereas in large boats replacement is usually a lot more costly than sistering. The number and location of frames needing repair affect this decision, too. Frames carrying high transverse loads, such as those over ballast or near engines, centerboards, or maststeps, are not good candidates for sister framing, since it is difficult to tie in sister frames to the floor timbers and deck where these loads originate. Less highly stressed frames in the ends of boats may respond better to sistering.

From a structural point of view, reframing by replacement is always the best route, but when the condition of the rest of the boat or the condition of the owner's finances preclude this solution, sister framing may be the most reasonable strategy.

But whichever method you choose, don't make the same mistake the last person did. If you are reasonably sure that your boat's frame problems are due to a design or construction deficiency, install the new or sister frames in such a way that frame breakage doesn't recur.

Situations and Solutions

Here are some hypothetical situations for which I've proposed solutions, along with some rationale to help you decide what to do in your particular situation, even if it's slightly different.

1–The old girl needs refastening again.
But the old fastenings won't come out easily or at all, and there's no more room in either the planking or in the frames for another set of fastenings. (Remember that fastenings are most effective near the edges of the planks, and that area has been all used up.) The second round of fastenings is often the coup de grace for bent frames, especially those in lightly built boats. The extra holes weaken the frames, which often break at places where the bend is more than moderately severe.

The best plan of attack here is to replace the frames, plugging extra holes in the planking so the new screws can be driven in the right places in the planks. However, if the condition of the rest of the boat doesn't warrant the expense of replacement, if the old frames aren't badly cracked, and if the hull still has its shape, it may be better to sister the frames and refasten into the sisters than to weaken the original frames by driving more fastenings. This method can add a lot more mileage to an old hull quite inexpensively; not only is the hull shape stiffened and stabilized, but also the old frames are a lot less likely to break afterwards and cause deformation. Conversely, weight is added, a lot of extra holes are put in the planking, and the boat is altered from the way it was originally built. For this method to be effective, the sister frames should extend all the way from the floor timbers to the sheer clamp.

2–The old girl needed refastening about 10 years ago but didn't get it.

This situation is similar to the last one, except that now the planks have started pulling away from the frames, the seams have opened up and have probably been recaulked in places, and it's likely that some of the frames are cracked badly enough to cause a loss of hull shape. There may be an accumulation of paint or debris, as well as additional caulking, in the openings where the planks and frames have begun to separate.

Again, reframing is the best course of action, and since there will be more than a few isolated frames involved, the job will be quite extensive. Once the planks start pulling away and the seams begin to open up, it's unlikely that sister framing will be able to pull things back together. And if the hull shape has been lost, it's almost impossible to restore and retain it by sistering. When things have reached this stage, it's also likely that the fastenings at the upper and lower ends of the frames, i.e., those to floor timbers and sheer, are starting to go. At this point, it's almost a sure bet that simply refastening into the old frames will not be a success.

If an entire reframing job is out of the question, consider replacing only those frames that are actually broken or cracked so badly that a kink has developed in the hull. This will restore the shape and bring together the open seams. In other places, where the planks have pulled away from the original frames but the hull shape is intact, reef out the seams to clean out any obstructions behind the existing frames, then install sister frames.

3–The boat has a few scattered cracked frames.

In this situation, sister framing may make the most sense. As long as the cracked frames aren't all in a line, and there has been no serious loss of shape at the cracks, new sister frames extending well above and below the damaged area should stabilize things. If there is a little bit of a kink in the hull next to a frame crack, don't try to bend the sister frame into the kink (remember the bend

severity discussion), or it will break there a few years down the road. If a frame has cracked under the bilge stringer, the sister frame will have to be a bit smaller in its molded dimension than the original so it, too, doesn't get damaged by contact with the stringer and eventually break.

4–External damage has broken and cracked a few frames; everything else is okay.

This is a situation similar to Number 3, and again sister framing may make sense, especially if it eliminates the need to tear out much of the interior to gain access. The sister should extend well past the damaged area in both directions (at least four or five planks in each direction from any detectable damage), and as a rule it should never end in the middle of a curve. If things are easily accessible, however, remember that replacing a few frames is not that big a job, and the boat will be as originally built with no extra weight or holes in the planking.

5–There are many small fractures, and possibly a few big ones, in a lot of frames through the turn of the bilge.

This problem is very common and is almost always caused by a design deficiency. The frames were either bent too severely or the fastenings were driven too closely to the edges, or both. If the boat is planked with mahogany, the problem may be that the frames are simply too small in cross section for that type of wood. The problem usually gets worse, eventually ending in complete fractures and loss of hull shape. The original fractures usually occur soon after the boat is built, and some may have even developed during construction. Frames against double planking may remain stable for a great many years after the initial cracking, as long as the frames' unsevered fibers provide the necessary strength. In such cases, the frames often eventually fail because of decay caused by moisture that has collected in the cracks.

If reframing is out of the question, sister framing may stabilize the boat almost indefinitely, provided there aren't any bad kinks in the hull or evidence of transverse tension loads on the planking as indicated by open seams and split planks. These sister frames may be placed in the middle of the frame bays except where butt blocks interfere. (Don't remove a butt block on the mistaken assumption that a sister frame down the middle of a frame bay will take its place.) Where there is a butt block, install the sister frame next to the original frame, cutting enough of the butt block away to let the sister frame pass by.

Sister frames should run at least from the

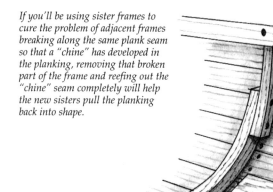

If you'll be using sister frames to cure the problem of adjacent frames breaking along the same plank seam so that a "chine" has developed in the planking, removing that broken part of the frame and reefing out the "chine" seam completely will help the new sisters pull the planking back into shape.

6–A number of adjacent frames are broken along the same plank seam, and a knuckle or "chine" has developed in the planking.

The only suitable way out of this problem is to remove and replace all the frames in the problem area. If there's a bilge stringer in the way (and if there is, more often than not it has contributed to the problem), it should be removed for access. If the frame broke behind the stringer, don't put the old stringer back in. Instead, use a wide, flat stringer, or several wide, flat strakes of ceiling.

If you go about the repair conservatively, removing and replacing one frame at a time, you'll probably find the unwanted knuckle is still there when you finish and that the new frames have conformed to the unfair spots rather than pulled the hull back into shape. The only way to treat such an extreme case is to take out a number of adjacent frames and at the same time completely reef out the offending "chine" seam so the planking can be drawn back in to its proper place. Before you fasten in a new frame in a situation like this, you should always remove at least a couple of frames between it and the old broken ones. An adjacent broken frame will retain its knuckle shape and prevent the planking from pulling in against a pre-bent fair frame. And when new frames are bent right into place in the boat, they have a tendency to duplicate any unfairness in the planking.

Of course, situations arise when a boat owner, faced with this frame problem, has no other choice but to "funk it out." In such a case, sister frames again come into the picture. However, if the unfair area is only sistered and no other changes are made, there won't be any improvement in shape, and the sisters are very likely to take the unfair, severely bent shape and break after a year or two.

There are two possible approaches to the problem. First, sister the frames, kerfing the sisters if necessary to ease the severity of the bend, and let the sisters line fairly over the hard spot, shimming behind them for solid fastenings. Second, cut back part of the original frames the width of several planks each way from the break, sister the frames, and pull the planks back into shape, letting the sisters do all the work of the original frames over

gently curving topsides to the flat area below the turn of the bilge. When the hull is single planked, frames cracked from severe bending usually deteriorate in time and completely break, and the fairness of the inside of the planking is lost. After this happens, sister framing must be considered a last-ditch stabilizing measure for a hull that really needs reframing — a measure that may be the only practical solution if the boat's overall condition is marginal.

Whether you replace broken frames or decide to sister them, you should make changes so the new frames or sisters don't develop the same problems. If the bend is too severe, you can ease it by decreasing the frame's molded dimension with a corresponding increase in its siding. But usually cutting saw kerfs in the frames before bending — thus halving the severity of the bend — is necessary. When the frames are too narrow to take fastenings properly, or when complete tension breaks indicate an insufficient frame cross section, an increase in sided dimension should accompany the kerfing. With the saw kerfs, the original molded dimension can be maintained

the problem area. If the unfair spot is under the bilge stringer, either of the above methods may be impossible without removing the stringer.

7–Frame heels are split or broken where they bend down into the bilge, but the rest of the frames are sound.

Here, the cause is almost always the severity of the bend. Known as the "Noviboat syndrome," the problem is very serious in ballasted sailboats. With split or broken heels, the frames are generally unable to carry the ballast load up into the hull above the floor timbers, resulting in split planks or opened-up garboard seams as the load falls on the planking. The only way to restore such a boat to its original strength is to replace each flawed frame entirely, eliminating the cause of the problem at the same time.

Where the frame heels are socketed into the keel,

Scantling Rules Used by Herreshoff and Nevins

These rules are a good guide to the relationships among displacement, plank thickness, and frame size and spacing. The frame scantlings listed in the table are the sided and molded dimensions below the turn of the bilge for frames square at that point.

Both builders adhered quite closely to their rules for plank thickness, frame spacing, and molded dimension, but both usually decreased the sided dimension considerably from the rule scantlings. Herreshoff tapered molded dimensions to about 85 percent of the rule dimension at the frame head, and Nevins to 110 percent or more of the rule dimension at the heel. Herreshoff also often tapered the sided dimension at the top for about one-third of the frame length, except in the way of hanging knees.

Herreshoff's rule provides for slightly thicker planking than does Nevins's; Herreshoff usually planked with softwood, whereas Nevins used a lot of mahogany.

Herreshoff's rule gives larger frame dimensions with greater spacing. In practice, Herreshoff generally used a sided dimension similar to that called for by Nevins's rule.

The table for frame cross section per lineal foot of hull shows that Herreshoff's rule produced a more heavily framed hull in the smaller sizes; Nevins's rule in the larger sizes. Herreshoff sometimes halved the frame spacing in way of the maststep. These values should be considered a minimum for single-planked mahogany boats, which often have problems with tension breaks in the frames because of the compressive strength of

$\sqrt[3]{D}$ (ft)	Displ. (lbs)	Thickness of Plank (in)	Frame Space (in)	Frame Siding/ Molding (in)	Frame Area (in²/ft of hull)
3.0	1,728	H .44	5.9	.80	1.31
		N .36	4.8	.64	1.02
3.5	2,744	H .52	6.8	.95	1.60
		N .46	5.4	.74	1.22
4.0	4,096	H .60	7.7	1.10	1.90
		N .56	6.0	.81	1.31
4.5	5,832	H .69	8.5	1.26	2.22
		N .64	6.7	.96	1.65
5.0	8,000	H .77	9.4	1.41	2.53
		N .72	7.4	1.13	2.07
5.5	10,648	H .86	10.2	1.56	2.88
		N .80	8.0	1.30	2.54
6.0	13,824	H .94	11.0	1.72	3.24
		N .90	8.7	1.48	3.02
6.5	17,576	H 1.03	11.9	1.88	3.57
		N .98	9.1	1.65	3.59
7.0	21,952	H 1.16	12.7	2.04	3.93
		N 1.08	10.0	1.83	4.02
8.0	32,768	H 1.29	14.3	2.36	4.69
		N 1.25	11.3	2.17	5.00
9.0	46,656	H 1.47	15.9	2.69	5.46
		N 1.43	12.5	2.50	6.00
10.0	64,000	H 1.65	17.5	3.02	6.26
		N 1.60	13.7	2.82	6.97
11.00	85,184	H 1.83	19.0	3.36	7.11
		N 1.76	14.9	3.15	7.99
12.00	110,592	H 2.02	20.6	3.69	7.94
		N 1.93	16.1	3.51	9.18

Values are for ballasted sailing craft. Frame sizes slightly less for centerboarders.

mahogany.

Although both builders recommend the use of saw kerfs in the tops of severely bent frames to ease the severity of bend, they rarely practiced what they preached, and boats of both builders have frame problems in areas of tight curvature for that reason.

it may be physically impossible to install a full-length replacement frame. Since the tight bend that was needed to get the frame heel into its socket in the first place probably caused the problem, it is usually preferable to abandon this technique in the repair. If the floor timbers are properly fastened to the ballast and backbone, and if the frames are properly connected to the floor timbers, socketing the frame heels gives little or no structural advantage. Cutting a saw kerf to ease the severity of the bend in the frame heels may compromise the effectiveness of the floor-to-frame fastenings.

A better, and in many cases only, strategy here is to let the frame run out onto the face of the floor timber. This eases the severity of the bend, makes full-length frame installation possible without removing any planking, and places the floor-to-frame fastenings inboard, away from the end-grain of the floor timber. The old frame can be cut off flush at the top of the keel if socketed, or, if not rotten, cut off higher so the new frame lies on top of it. Where the new frame is close to the planking but not in contact, wedges can be inserted between frame and plank to allow solid fastening. Where the new frame runs well away from the planking, the plank fastenings can go into the floor timber, into the bottom of the old frame if it's still here, or into a sawn cleat fastened to the edge of the floor timber for this purpose.

Boats built by Herreshoff never had socketed frames, and, in many cases, the fastenings in the lower planks went only into the floor timbers, because the frames ran out onto the floor-timber faces as described above. Of course, longer screws should generally be used where the plank fastenings go into the end-grain of the floors.

In very mild cases of frame-heel splitting, where the splits haven't loosened the floor-to-frame fastenings, a metal strap on top of the frame will keep matters from getting any worse by holding the splits from lifting. If the splitting is more serious, but you can't replace the top part of the frame for financial reasons, you can bend in a new bottom part of the frame, preferably in place of the old one, with a scarf joint connecting it to the original top. This joint should be located where the frame has little curvature, with metal splice plates fastened on one side and on top of the joint to allow transfer of tension, and a sister frame next to the joint, fastened to both pieces of the frame.

In summary, frame replacement is always the best repair method from a structural viewpoint, and although more expensive initially than sister framing, it is usually more economical in the long run. In certain situations, however, sister framing is suitable, particularly when the boat has other serious problems that make the expense of reframing impractical.

Footnote:

Many people seem to think that kerfing frames is bad. The boatbuilder who can torture a poor frame into bending whole often looks down on the guy who "takes the easy way out," i.e., uses a kerf. People who repair boats look at things a little differently. I've been replacing and sistering frames for more than 10 years, and I can't remember seeing a kerfed frame that failed without external abuse. Some of the best people in the business kerfed frames when they thought it necessary. Herreshoff, Nevins, and Bud McIntosh did. (Herreshoff, however, only kerfed extremely severe bends; the moderately severe ones that he didn't kerf provide jobs for people like me.)

Bending Wood

by Richard Jagels

My neighbor made an ox-yoke about a half century ago. The oxen are gone but the yoke still hangs in his barn. What particularly impresses me is the pristine condition of the bows. I have seen many yokes, but all too often I have observed wood separation on the outer surface of the sharp bend. On close examination I found that my neighbor had left the bark on his hickory bows. He said his father told him that good tight bark on the outside of the bend prevented splitting.

Jim Steele's jig for bending peapod stems. The steamed wood is bent over a form, while a steel strap presses tightly against the entire outside surface.

Restraining the Tension Surface

Controlled tests of the bending characteristics of steam-plasticized wood by various testing laboratories have confirmed the importance of restraining the tension surface. Plasticized wood can be compressed as much as 25 to 30 percent but can be stretched only .05 percent before failure occurs.

Tight bark on wood to be bent has now been generally replaced with a steel tension strap with end fittings. The strap presses tightly against the outside of the bend as the end fittings force the entire piece of wood into compression. As the wood is bent the strap bears the tensile stress normally developed on the outer surface of the curve. When bending oak, an interlayer of aluminum or other nonferrous metal is used between the strap and the wood to avoid discoloration caused by the reaction of iron with tannic acid.

— 11 —

Steam Pressure

Steaming at atmospheric pressure seems to be the universally preferred method for softening or plasticizing wood for bending, although boiling the wood in water is an acceptable alternative. Recommended heating times of 30 to 45 minutes per inch thickness of the wood holds for stock that has a moisture content of 20 to 25 percent. If the wood is drier than this, steaming time must be increased to one hour or more per inch thickness.

High-pressure steaming has been tried but has proven unsatisfactory. Prolonged steaming also seems to have deleterious effects. Green wood can be bent without steaming, but two disadvantages weigh against the procedure:

(1) Water fills the wood cells and when compressed ruptures the cell walls, significantly weakening the wood.

(2) The wood, once bent, may severely warp or twist as it dries unless securely restrained.

Plasticizing agents other than heated water have been tried with varying degrees of success. Urea and methyl urea have been used in a limited way commercially. Liquid ammonia is a highly effective (and patented) plasticizing agent — wood treated with it can be bent or twisted into complex curves by hand — but the expensive apparatus required in its use and the toxicity of ammonia limit its usefulness.

Bending Properties of Wood

Why do some woods have superior bending properties than others, and why are hardwoods superior to most softwoods? I weighed these questions recently and concluded that at least three wood properties are essential for steam or hot water bending:

(1) The wood must be porous or open-grained so heat and moisture can be thoroughly and evenly distributed.

(2) The wood must have superior strength properties, especially in bending.

(3) The wood should have a high cellulose-to-lignin ratio. (Cellulose is plasticized by water, while lignin — the "glue" that holds the wood cells together — is water resistant and accounts for rigidity in wood.)

This last characteristic is the probable reason why conifers (or softwoods) are, on the whole, difficult to bend. Such species contain a high propor-

Wood Characteristics Favorable to Bending

Species	Large Pores in Earlywood	Numerous Pores in Growth Rings	Interlocked Grain	Strength (especially impact bending)
Elm	yes	yes	yes	high
Hackberry*	yes	yes	yes	high
Oak	yes	varies	no	high
Ash	yes	no	no	high
Sassafras**	yes	no	no	—
Hickory	yes	no	no	very high
Persimmon***	sometimes	no	no	—
Black Locust	yes	varies	no	high
Southern Magnolia	no	yes	no	moderate
Sweetgum	no	yes	yes	high
Black Gum (Tupelo)	no	yes	yes	moderate
Beech	no	often	sometimes	high
Birch	no	sometimes	no	high
Maple	no	sometimes	no	low to high
Mahogany (Honduras & African)	no	no	usually	high
Walnut	sometimes	no	no	high
Sycamore	no	yes	often	low
Willow	no	yes	occasionally	low
Red Alder	no	yes	no	low
Cherry	no	yes	no	moderate
Holly	no	yes	no	—
Dogwood	no	varies	no	—

*often marketed with elm   **often marketed with black ash   ***often marketed with hickory

tion of lignin, especially in the latewood. The one conifer that bends reasonably easily is Alaska yellow cedar, which has almost no latewood. Experiments in bending Southern yellow pine at the Southern Forest Experiment Station, Pineville, Louisiana, further corroborate the significance of lignin-saturated latewood. The Pineville experiments showed that low-density pine with a high percentage of earlywood had a significantly lower failure rate when bent than high-density pine with wide bands of latewood.

Analyzing Bending Properties

As a test for my hypothetical bending properties, I decided to draw up a list of hardwoods, including in it those woods known to bend readily as well as some more resistant to bending, and plot strength and porosity to determine if these properties were indeed correlated with ease of bending. In making the list I stumbled upon another property that seemed important — interlocked grain. This property is undoubtedly most valuable in preventing failure on the tension surface of the wood. In my table I have omitted cellulose-to-lignin ratios, because data was not at hand and ratios vary considerably from tree to tree depending on growth rate and environmental factors. Porosity is divided into two columns. One accounts for those woods with large earlywood pores (ring-porous woods), and the other documents those woods that may lack large springwood pores but which contain numerous pores throughout the growth ring.

By good fortune (or perhaps, an unconscious bias on my part) elm and hackberry — the two woods traditionally placed at the top of bending lists — are the only two woods that exhibit all the positive properties I have suggested. From the table you can pick out your favorite wood and see how well it fits, or you can check out these properties for other woods you might wish to try bending.

In using a table such as this, one has to decide which of the characteristics to rank as more important for a particular use. If final strength of the bentwood member is of little importance, then willow might be an adequate choice. Unfortunately, frames and stems in boats, the members most usually bent, generally require high impact strength.

Another, more-subtle pitfall concerns porosity. If a wood contains an excessively large number of pores encompassed by thin-walled vessels, strength properties may be diminished somewhat: thus, one property may be enhanced at the expense of another. Elm and hackberry seem to have compensated for large and numerous pores with interlocked

grain to retain high bending strength.

The number of pores per unit area in birch and maple is highly variable. Some specimens will have numerous pores, while others will have few. This may account for the variability of bending ease often associated with these woods. Prolonged steaming of low-porosity specimens may help, but experienced "woodwarpers" agree that extended steaming generally leads to unsatisfactory results. In fact, the Pineville, Louisiana, researchers found that 10 to 20 minutes per inch thickness of Southern pine was sufficient; longer steaming times resulted in greater tension and compression failure.

They also tested another variable often overlooked in bending: the possible effect of grain orientation; i.e., whether the lumber is flat-sawn or quarter-sawn. For Southern pine they found that quarter-sawn lumber yielded a higher percentage of bending success — twice as many quarter-sawn pieces were acceptable than were flat-sawn. No differences could be found between flat-sawn wood bent toward the pith side, or toward the bark side of the board. Not all this data on pine may be directly applicable to hardwoods, but it is worth consideration.

Quite aside from grain orientation, the tension and compression stresses imposed on wood during bending mandate the absence of any defects. Boards should be carefully selected for straight grain free from knots, pith, shake, decay, surface checks, case hardening, or any other irregularities imposed by God or man.

III

An Unpressured Approach to Steaming

—————by Edward F. McClave—————

Steaming equipment has a simple purpose: to raise the wood to the proper bending temperature (100 degrees C or 212 degrees F) all the way through, to avoid drying it out in the process, and to do this without harming the boatbuilder and at the least possible cost. Beyond fulfilling these requirements, any time or money spent on elaborate equipment is wasted, in my opinion.

Causes of Wood Breakage
The idea is to get wood to bend without breaking. The breakage of wood during the bending process can almost always be traced to one of four causes:

(1) The wood wasn't heated to the proper temperature.

(2) The grain of the wood wasn't straight enough. This can be a result of a tapered butt log being sawn improperly — parallel to centerline instead of the right way, parallel to the bark — or of improper stock selection or preparation by the boatbuilder.

(3) The wood was too dry.

(4) The builder attempted to bend the wood to a more severe curve than was appropriate for the species.

Steam Pressure
Many steam-generating rigs, including some shown in Chapter 5, are capable of building up steam pressure. Steam under any pressure, even slightly above atmospheric pressure, is extremely dangerous, and there's no reason to even consider using pressurized steam for any boatbuilding operation. Steam

under pressure is so dangerous, in fact, that it's illegal in most places for unlicensed people to play around with it. (Everyone knows that you can pass your hand quickly through a 3,000-degree-F flame without harm; try the same trick with a 212-degree-F live-steam jet, and you will literally lose your skin.)

Besides overriding safety concerns, there are other disadvantages to steaming under pressure. In fact, bending tests performed by the Forest Products Laboratory of the U.S. Department of Agriculture have shown that no advantage is gained, either in allowing more severe bends or in success rate, by the use of pressurized (high-temperature) steam.

When a stick steaming at a temperature above 212 degrees F, which can only be achieved by using a pressure greater than atmospheric, is suddenly brought into the atmosphere and depressurized, the excess heat contained in the stick can cause the wood at and near the surface to dry excessively and rapidly as the pressure decreases to atmospheric, creating damaging checks at the stick's surface. Another problem is that wet wood begins to break down chemically at temperatures above the normal boiling point. Pressure is neither necessary nor desirable to plasticize wood for bending.

Steam Box Design
Steam-generating equipment and steam boxes can be designed to be perfectly effective while also making pressure buildup impossible. The only pressure necessary is that required to move the steam from the boiling can to the steam box — in

other words, a fraction of one psi above atmospheric pressure. To avoid excessive pressure, the hose from the boiling can to the box should be reasonably large, and there should be no attempt made in the design or construction of the box to make it hold steam pressure.

If steam is generated in a boiler such as a kerosene can, simply replacing the screw cap on the can's fill fitting with a softwood plug will ensure that very little pressure can be generated. If the boiling can can't hold pressure, there's no possibility of there being any appreciable pressure in the box. Just to be sure, however, a simple friction-fit steam box door with no latch is the easiest and most efficient arrangement.

Steam Temperature

While it's not advisable to operate steam boxes at pressures above atmospheric pressure and correspondingly elevated temperatures, it is highly desirable to keep the temperature of the wood as close as possible to the boiling point. This can be done quite effectively without resorting to pressure.

Wood bends more easily at 212 degrees F than at 200 degrees F or even 205 degrees F. Because maintaining the proper temperature is critical, a steam box thermometer is a necessity. A metal meat thermometer, stuck into a small hole at the coolest place in the steam box — as far from the steam inlet and as low as possible — will do the trick. Although the numbered scales of most meat thermometers stop at about 180 degrees F, many have a calibration mark at exactly the boiling point. The temperature in the box should be within 10 degrees F of this mark for most of the steaming period, and it should be right on the mark for the last 10 minutes or so before any stick is removed for bending.

In conclusion, if builders put more effort in getting straight-grained wood and less into constructing overly elaborate steam boxes, they would break fewer frames. Broken frames and expensive steaming rigs both raise the cost of the finished product.

IV

A Steam Box Primer

*I*n every one of the boatbuilding classes I teach, the students at some point have to make a contraption for steam-bending wood. Each rig is different, and I've had to develop a keen sense of what is likely to work and what isn't. Some events simply cannot be foreseen — like the time we had to have our hot little blaze extinguished by local volunteer firemen.

If you've had any difficulty steam-bending wood, you can usually pin it on one or more of the following: the source of heat, the boiler, the steam box itself, the bending stock, or your bending techniques.

Heat

Many people have an image in their minds of steam penetrating the wood and softening it. This is not so. The steam only heats the internal moisture of the wood, causing it to become supple; it also surrounds the wood with 100 percent humidity so it cannot dry out.

Live steam is an invisible gas. What you see is condensed water vapor that has already lost some of its usefulness. To get live steam in quantity requires a powerful heat source. The few times I've had to use a single-burner Coleman stove, a Primus, an electric hot plate, or a rented electric wallpaper steamer, the results have been marginal at best.

What I've found does work are: scrap-wood fires in steel barrels; multi-burner sources of heat (an electric range with two or more burners, for example); a kerosene or propane gas plumber's stove (used for melting lead); and commercial, outdoor propane-fired grills.

Boiler

Obviously, the boiler must be strong enough to stand the heat, but there are two additional requirements. First, the boiler should hold enough water for at least an hour's steaming. Second, it must be rigged so water can be added as necessary without interrupting the flow of steam more than very briefly. If you are using electric heat, you'll save money by insulating the boiler with fiberglass batting. One of the most widely available boilers is a 10-gallon bucket with a tightfitting lid and a 1½-inch screw cap.

Steam Box

The box itself should be connected to the boiler with a large-diameter pipe, 1 inch or more, kept as short as possible. Watch out that you don't use some thermoplastic material that may melt — I've had this happen. Take care also that the steam box is not so close to the flames that it will catch fire; otherwise you might end up with barbecued ribs instead of steamed ones.

Keep the box as small as is consistent with the length and number of the timbers you're steaming. If it's too long, shorten it by stuffing a burlap bag down the inside. Devise a door at one end that is

— 17 —

tight but that can be quickly opened and closed.

I usually drill the hole for the steam pipe up through the bottom near the middle of the box. To conserve hot water, slope the floor of the box toward the hole so condensate drains back into the boiler.

Be sure to make some kind of internal rack so the wood is off the floor of the box. One way is to run pieces of ½- or ¾-inch dowel through the sides of the box. If you have a marginal heat source, insulate the box with fiberglass. You'll find it takes about an hour to heat up the box; the smaller and the better-insulated the box, the less time it will take to get hot.

Steaming

An hour in the box — after it is itself hot — for each inch of thickness of your wood is a pretty good rule. My hunch is that there is an optimum steaming time that depends upon the size, type, quality, and moisture content of the wood. Cook the wood too long, and it gets brittle and is more apt to break. How do you know when the wood is ready? You (with gloves on, of course) pull a piece out of the box and try flexing it. It should feel heavy and limp — sort of floppy. Test it to see how readily it will take the bend you want.

Wood

It is crucial to choose a species of wood that is amenable to steaming. The stock must be free from even the smallest knots and have straight grain — or almost so. If I see the grain lines departing from the centerline of the timber by more than 5 to 10 degrees, I discard it.

Equally important is the moisture content of bending stock. Just as you can't have too much steam, you cannot have wood that is too green. In one class in Michigan, we cut a small locust tree in the morning, steamed it, and bent it into the boat in the afternoon.

I always coat the wood to be steamed with boiled linseed oil and wipe the surplus off immediately. This helps hold the heat while bending and prevents the surface from drying out so rapidly that it checks, or develops splits.

Leave the frames at least 20 inches longer than their final length so there will be enough left over at each end to grip. Even with good bending stock, allow at least one-third more wood than you will need. It's a good plan to mark the center of each piece with a crayon, so you can find the center in a hurry.

Bending Dry Stock

Trying to bend dry wood is asking for trouble. However, if you cannot get green stock, you may recover some bending ability by soaking the wood. Cut the wood a shade over its finished size and soak it in heavily salted water for at least a month. This may work for air-dried stock, but kiln-dried wood is more stubborn. If that's what you're stuck with, you'd do better to glue-laminate all the frames, using the boat itself as a form, and forget about trying to bend solid ones.

Framing

Framing must be done quickly, so everything should be made ready beforehand. If you are going to use nails or rivets to fasten the frames to the planks, then all the nails should be started through the planking first. Make certain you won't run out of water or fire in the middle of the operation. Get enough people to help — at least three, including yourself — and then have a few dry runs. Start in the middle of the boat and work toward the wider end, then the narrower. Try to get the nails in the middle third of the frames. If they start to split, you may have to bend them in place, clamp them until cool, then come back and drill holes for the nails.

If a frame shows any sign of cracking, don't fuss with it; rip it out, call for another, and keep going. If all goes well, you can frame a 14-foot boat in less than an hour. As one Nova Scotian boatbuilder liked to say, " 'Tis eager work."

A Steam Box Scrapbook

by Karl MacKeeman

*T*o modify an old saying, there is more than one way to build a steam box for bending wood. Here is a collection of home-designed steam boxes, most built from materials at hand; all, to a greater or lesser extent, have been useful.

Please note that the publisher does not recommend any particular steam box, rig, or method, nor does it certify the safety or effectiveness of any of the boxes and boilers included here. The intention is to indicate the wide range of possibilities, and the imagination, resourcefulness, and, occasionally, fearlessness of wooden boat builders. Which suggests this caution:

Steaming wood can be a risky business. The procedure involves fire, boiling water, high pressures, scaldingly-hot steam, hot timbers, and other potential hazards. Please, please be careful, and be sure to follow proper safety standards and any codes established by your community.

The Well-Placed Window
by Terry Ridings

To help dispel the myth that steam-bending wood requires lots of fancy equipment, here is a description of the system that I used for restoring *Chloe*, a 14-foot lapstrake dinghy. Not everyone will be as fortunate as I with the design of their house, however. Ours allowed for the steam generator to sit on a burner of the kitchen stove, with the end of the steam box poking out the window, which just happens to be about 6 feet from the carport, where I was working on the boat. The steam generator was a one-gallon, metal, white-gas container turned on its side, and the box was an old PVC rainwater pipe, about 2 ½ inches in diameter. Both of these items were found in the garden shed. The coupling that connected the steam generator to the steam box was made from a short length of garden hose, bits of rag, and some duct tape.

This system successfully steamed the 12 new ribs needed in the boat, but it had to be upgraded to a larger-diameter aluminum rainwater pipe (also found in the shed; I really must clean out that shed!) for steaming the false keel.

The Flexible Steam Box
by J.W. England, Jr.

Here we have a discarded water tank set up on cinder blocks. A piece of 2-inch-diameter exhaust hose leads from the outlet of the tank to a piece of 4-inch-diameter flexible plastic drainpipe. The joint is taped with duct tape, and the end is plugged with rags. The pipe is laced to a 2 by 4, and supported by a 6-foot stepladder on one end and a post, to which it is clamped, on the other. The post, in turn, is clamped to a sawhorse.

Add 10 gallons of water to the tank, throw a good pile of dry wood scraps into the fire under it, and this rig really cooks.

When this photograph was taken, we were steaming new oak sheerstrakes for a Herreshoff 12½-footer. The flexible drainpipe allowed for the curved shape of each piece, which had already been spiled and cut to length. We fully expected the pipe to disintegrate, but it didn't.

We have subjected the pipe to hot steam for up to two hours with no apparent damage. The rags blew out one time because we allowed the rig to get too hot, but otherwise our steam box worked well.

Steam Boxes for a Lyle Hess Cutter
by Ken and Mo Fraser

We used several types of steam boxes during the building of our 29-foot Lyle Hess cutter. For steaming frames, we used the traditional long box made of cedar and wrapped in pink insulation and set on sawhorses. The steam was supplied by a propane roofing torch that heated water in a salvaged 20-gallon hot-water tank.

For steaming planking, we used a 10-foot piece of 6-inch-diameter ABS black plastic sewer pipe in which we drilled a ½-inch hole in the middle. When the planking was planed and ready to be offered up, we clamped a plank in place at each frame until it no longer could be comfortably bent dry. Then we put our pipe-steam box over the free end of the plank, plugged both ends of the box with rags, and inserted a 10-foot length of ½-inch black-plastic water hose into the hole that we had drilled into the middle of the pipe. The hose was connected to an 18-inch length of copper pipe brazed to the side of a war-surplus jerry can. The can, full of water, was set up on bricks and heated with a propane torch to produce steam. After steaming, we quickly removed the pipe-steam box and clamped the hot plank in place. We allowed the plank to cool and set before fastening.

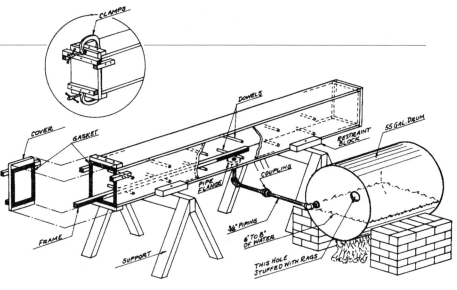

The Classic Wooden Steam Box
by Joseph P. Perry

I wanted an efficient, easy-to-build box to steam the ⅞- by ⅞-inch white oak frames for my 19-foot Charles Mower-designed Petrel daysailer. And since the steam box was to be used only once, I didn't want to spend a lot of money on it.

I used four 1-inch by 10-inch by 11-foot pine boards. The length was governed by the longest frames — in Petrel's case, about 9 feet. Stacking the two side panels of the box, I drilled holes for ½-inch dowels through both boards at two levels and about 18 inches apart. The side panels were then mounted on the bottom of the box, and ½-inch dowels were pushed through the holes across the box; they would be used as shelves for the framing stock. The top and rear boards were then installed. All joints were laid in a strand of caulking and fastened with closely spaced 8-penny nails.

For the front end, I chose to make a loose cover that could be closed tightly against the box with two C-clamps. To seal the cover I stapled lengths of common weatherstripping around the edges of the opening and on the mating surfaces inside the cover.

For a boiler, I obtained a free 55-gallon oil drum from a local service station. It was laid on its side on a temporary fireplace made of loose bricks to provide about 12 inches under the drum for a fire. The drum end had two threaded holes, one that was ¾-inch in diameter, and a larger one that was stuffed with rags during steaming to maintain some pressure. The smaller hole was very convenient for a ¾-inch pipe that connected the drum to the bottom of the box. I had some old ½-inch house piping left over from a plumbing renovation and was able to adapt it, using a ¾- by ½-inch bushing at the drum. I had to buy only the bushing and a pipe flange to mount on the bottom of the box under a ½-inch-diameter hole drilled into the box for steam entry.

About 6 to 8 inches of water was added to the drum with a garden hose through the larger opening. With a hot fire, it wasn't long before a good head of steam built up in the box. Then the frames were put in. After about an hour of steaming, the frames were taken out and bent like rubber hose inside the hull. Out of a total of about 50 pieces of frame stock, we broke only five or six.

Plastic Sewer Pipe with a Touch of Elegance
by C. Greg Rössel

A quick, off-the-shelf solution for a steam box suitable for bending long, thin stock is a heavy-duty plastic sewer pipe. It can be easily cut, or lengthened with the use of couplings. The plastic seems to hold the heat, and it is extremely tight — so tight, in fact, that it is necessary to drill vent holes along the bottom of the pipe-steam box to avoid untimely explosion from pressure build-up. It is good to install horizontal support wires across the diameter of the pipe to hold up your stock inside the pipe for full steam exposure. Copper wire or clothes-hanger wire works well; iron wire will leave black lines on your stock.

I recommend placing an oak support lengthwise under the pipe to prevent it from wilting in the heat. For a touch of class, a meat thermometer can be installed, its probe poked though a hole drilled in the top of the pipe.

A hot plate that runs off propane is my heat source; a new kerosene can is my boiler. I use an automobile

heater hose to connect the can to a reducer coupling screwed onto one end of the steam box. I close off the other end with a cap threaded into a coupling that is screwed to the sewer pipe.

A Simple Solution
by Ronald Hearon

My steam box is made from an old, discarded 14-inch-diameter galvanized-steel water tank. I cut off one end with a circular saw, using an abrasive cutoff blade. Firebrick makes up the firebox. Fuel is scrap wood from the shop.

I start out by pouring about 5 gallons of water into the tank. About an hour after I build the fire, I have to pour in another gallon. In my latest steam box, I drilled a drain hole at the proper water level so I could keep an eye on it better.

To steam ribs for my 21-foot Muscongus Bay sloop, I built a wooden rack that slides into the steam box. The box can hold about 10 ribs at a time. Burlap bags are laid loosely over the end of the tank to contain the steam.

For steaming long stock, two old water tanks of the same diameter can be welded together to attain the desired length.

The Stovepipe Steamer
by Walter Baron

I use this small steam box for bending canoe parts or other small parts. It has a lead-melting pot for the burner, a l-gallon tea kettle for the steam generator, and a length of ¼-inch plastic tubing inserted into the kettle with an adapter fashioned from the cap of a spray can of CRC. The tubing connects the kettle to a length of galvanized stovepipe, which is the steam box itself. The stovepipe has a cedar plug in one end with a hole in it for the tubing. When I needed some extra length, I added another piece of stovepipe (in a larger diameter because that was the only other piece I had) and used a burlap bag as a gasket. The box is partly lashed to the stepladder and partly hung from the roof trusses of the shop. I have used it to bend ribs for a 15-foot Walt Simmons-designed lapstrake canoe, and to bend flat ribs for a 17-foot Chestnut canoe I was rebuilding when this photograph was taken.

The box comes apart and is stored easily.

The Feather-Ruffler
by Ralph C. Wernett

While replacing the transom on my boat, I realized that to make a 3½-inch compound bend using two pieces of 3-inch by 3½-inch by 7-foot oak, I had to do some serious steaming. I came across some 4½-inch I.D. steel pipe when I was renovating a building and decided that it would work just fine to fit my needs for a steamer. I took an 11-foot section, cut off 3 feet, and welded the 3-foot section to the remaining 8 feet to form an "L." I covered the end of the long section of the L with a gallon pail stuffed with rags, propped it up to use as a steaming chamber, and rigged a bungee cord from the pail to the prop to act as a safety pressure release valve. All I needed now were a few gallons of water poured into the short end of the L and a fire built under it. It took about an hour and a lot of scrap wood to build a good head of steam.

A word of caution: Aim this steam box away from your neighbors; the looks of it can ruffle some feathers!

The Balchur Boiler
by Christian Blümel

For a steam box rig for my 35-foot Colin Archer, I used a Balchur, an oven made of sawdust, earth, and clay. Inside was an iron expansion tank from a central-heating system, which I found in a junkyard. It held about 10 gallons of water. This wasn't enough

water to heat up the 25-foot-long steam box, so the tank had to be refilled while the water was boiling. For this, I used rainwater out of two barrels.

The end of the steam box was filled with old clothes, so the planks could be longer than the box. The big oven with its thick walls kept the water boiling even when there was no fire below. This was important because when my friend and I got stuck working with a complicated plank, we had no time to look after the fire.

A Cadillac of Steam Generators
by J. Murray Abercrombie

Until the early 1980s, I generated steam for my steam box with a conventional boiler made from a hot-water tank. It took an hour or so to get up steam and required fairly regular tending to keep the water level up and the woodbox filled, but I thought it was reasonably efficient and somehow fitting to burn old wood and scraps to develop steam to bend new wood.

While rebuilding a 40-foot camp tender, though, I pondered this method and decided that there must be an easier way. And so was built the prototype of the steam generator I am currently using. It was made from regular black stovepipe, copper tubing, a few miscellaneous valves and fittings, and a couple of pieces of flat steel bar. This prototype lasted about six years and the building of a lot of boats; it has since been replaced by a "Cadillac" built of stainless steel at a cost of about $130 (1989 prices).

Two stainless-steel pipes are fitted together to create the generator. A 46-inch pipe, 5 inches in diameter, sits inside a wider, 36-inch-long stainless-steel pipe, 7 inches in diameter. The tops of the pipes should be bolted together to maintain the space between them, or they can be through-bolted with Redirod. The bottoms of the pipes can be spaced as part of the leg assembly.

Water is supplied by a garden hose and is metered through a needle valve cracked open approximately one-eighth turn. After passing through the valve, water enters a coil of ⅛-inch copper tubing 30 to 40 feet long, wound to fit inside the inner pipe of the boiler. A regular propane plumber's burner, mounted through a stovepipe cleanout cap that just fits the outer pipe on the bottom of the boiler, heats the water in the copper coil. Near the top of the outer pipe, the coil connects to a steam hose that leads to the steam box.

A wire clip attached to the generator body allows the burner to be removed easily for igniting. The burner is run with the valve and regulator fully open. Before entering the burner, air is preheated when it passes between the outer and inner pipes.

If there is no interruption in the water or

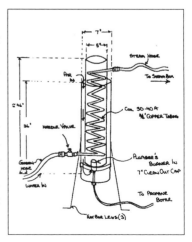

propane supplies, this boiler will operate all day without tending at a cost of about $1.05 per hour(1989). From ignition to steam takes about 10 to 15 seconds. When everything is fine tuned and at operating temperature, full efficiency is reached in about 1½ minutes. From then on, an occasional glance is all that is required.

The Steam Retort
from the J.S. Richardson Co.

Probably the ultimate in steaming sophistication, the Type S Steam Retort is manufactured by the J.S. Richardson Company of Sheboygan Falls, Wisconsin. Made of cast aluminum, the Type S delivers moist, pressurized steam throughout its standard 52-inch length. Steam is generally supplied from an industrial steam-generating unit, such as a high-pressure boiler. The pressure is reduced to about 3 pounds per square inch before it enters the retort. An automatic steam valve shuts off the flow of steam when the retort door is opened. The door is fitted with a molded rubber gasket to prevent leaks. Raised ribs in the bottom of the retort keep the stock from becoming stained by condensate, and the level of condensate is controlled automatically. If 52 inches isn't long enough for your wood-bending project, additional 25-inch sections can be bolted together and attached to the retort to make it longer.

According to William H. Richardson, Jr., the Thompson Boat Co. in Wisconsin used Richardson steam retorts, as did Chris-Craft in Florida. Today, users of Type S retorts include the Dunphy Boat Co. of Oshkosh, Wisconsin; the U.S. Naval Base at San Diego, California; the San Francisco Municipal Railway (for cable car restoration); and Amish wagon builders in Lancaster County, Pennsylvania.

Project Steam Box
by Steve Mayes

When friends saw our "Project Steam Box," they accused us of housing a hillbilly still, but it worked well for the ribs of a 36-foot Herreshoff Nereia. We used four long timbers, 2 inches by 12 inches by 12 feet, for the box. A hole was cut in the boat shed, and the box was inserted 6 inches to make it convenient to the final resting place of the oak frames. A hole was drilled in the middle of the top of the box, and a 1-inch pipe nipple was installed for the steam inlet hose. Originally, this was attached to a 13-gallon barrel that was set on bricks and heated with a tiger torch. When an 85-year-young boatbuilder/friend arrived, he suggested using his proper steam boiler. It was 2.9 hp — one-tenth more horse, and it would have required a qualified, ticketed operator. We hooked it up and got it heating with some scrap wood.

The first trial run of steam produced an unfamiliar and frightening noise, which was the superior supply of vapor roaring into the box, then out into the shed to find its escape route through an opening in the gable end of the roof, 15 feet overhead. A hinged door was affixed to the open end of the box in the shed, and all was ready for business. The framing was completed with only 6 out of 66 frames causing the air to turn blue.

Rube Goldberg
by D.W. Rolstone

Except for the box itself, my system was made from scrap lying around the workshop. The fire-box is an old French gas cylinder with a 4-inch steel pipe welded to it for a chimney, providing a good draw. Suspended inside is an old copper back boiler from a woodstove. This is connected to a gallon can with an open top so the water level can be seen and maintained. Because there is a constant exchange of water between the boiler and the can, with the condensate from the lower end of the box draining back into the can, the can and the connecting hose should be insulated. If the can is well insulated, the water in it can be kept nearly boiling.

The steam box is made from 1-inch spruce boards caulked, then nailed together and mounted at a slight angle. The steam is conducted from the boiler inside the gas cylinder to the center of the box by a 1-inch rubber hose.

Using wood offcuts, 20 minutes are required to raise steam. The system holds 2 gallons of water. Once running, the box builds up pressure, which raises the water level in the can. As long as cold water is added in small amounts to replace losses, the water will stay on the boil for hours, using a small amount of wood.

The heat of the fire and the amount of the draw is regulated with a piece of aluminum placed over the fire door.

Grounds for Divorce?
by R.L. Elton

I used a mortar casing set on top of the kitchen stove to steam new frames for my 1940 GarWood.

To bend the 1¼-inch oak transom boards, a 6-foot wooden steam box made from 1- by 12-inch boards was set on top of the kitchen stove. It worked very well, with rock salt added to the water. After they were steamed, the boards were taken out and clamped onto the boat. After they cooled and dried, they fit perfectly.

The key to this successful venture was my wife's best copper-bottomed pot, which I used for the steamer.

Yes, we're still married.

WoodenBoat School Steam Box
by Rich Hilsinger

Our boxes, 6-feet and 10-feet long, are made of 1 by 12 spruce fastened with drywall screws and clamped together with threaded rod and cleats about every 2 feet on the exterior. The rods keep the boxes tight and prevent them from racking. For steaming long stock, the boxes fit together. At 2-foot intervals, dowels run through the sides to accommodate various sizes of stock and to allow steam to flow freely around all the stock. There are removable doors at both ends of the boxes.

We use propane gas to fire a torch that heats up a 25-gallon copper hot-water tank, which is connected to the steam box by 1¼-inch threaded pipe. A threaded fitting allows us to fill the water tank and check the water level with a dipstick. A galvanized cover placed over the water tank blocks the wind and retains heat around the tank.

Postscript
by D.W. Stoner

Once I needed to bend some small-dimensioned strips of white oak, so I worked up a small-scale steam box using an old metal mailbox and a tea kettle. I simply heated water in the tea kettle on an electric stove and directed the steam out the spout through a small hole in the bottom of one end of the mailbox. It worked rather well.

Unfortunately, I never took a picture of this Rube Goldberg-like affair; the tea kettle was burned, and the mailbox was left behind on the last move.

VI

Reframing a Yacht

——— by Edward F. McClave with drawings by Sam Manning ———

T he winter of 1912-13 saw the construction of the nine yachts of the New York Fifty class at the Herreshoff yard in Bristol, Rhode Island. They were long, low, skinny, and deep, and for the next 70 years would be regarded as the quintessential "big" sailing yachts from Herreshoff's.

These sailing projectiles measured 72 feet overall, 50 feet on the waterline, 14 feet 6 inches in breadth, and 9 feet 9 inches in draft. The 50s started out as gaff sloops, but because this rig called for a large crew, all the boats were soon converted to more easily handled schooners, yawls, or marconi sloops. Several had illustrious racing careers under their new rigs.

L. Francis Herreshoff wrote that the 50s "were of about the finest material and workmanship that ever went into yachts of their size, and they were so efficiently built that...they only cost approximately $17,000 in 1913."

The 50s had a Universal-Rule-type hull: narrow, with low topsides, fairly slack bilges, and a short, heavy keel. Displacement was 74,900 pounds, and the ballast was 36,700 pounds. The hull was of conventional wood construction, builtlightly consider-

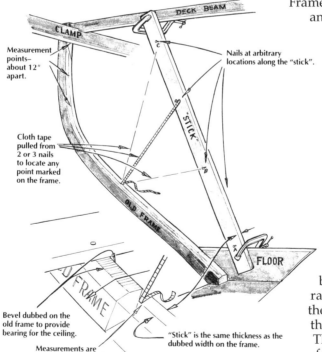

1a – Getting the Shape—

Measurement points— about 12" apart.

Cloth tape pulled from 2 or 3 nails to locate any point marked on the frame.

Nails at arbitrary locations along the "stick".

Bevel dubbed on the old frame to provide bearing for the ceiling.

Measurements are taken to the inboard edge of the bevel.

"Stick" is the same thickness as the dubbed width on the frame.

ing the size of the boat, with bent-oak frames 2 ½ inches square at the head, tapering to 2⅞ inches (sided) by 3½ inches (molded) at the heel. Floor timbers were of oak, plank-on-edge type, the largest 4 inches thick and over 3 feet deep.

Frames were on 18-inch centers, and there was a floor timber fastened to each pair, tying them together across the top of the keel.

The bottom was conventionally planked with 1 ¾-inch yellow pine, the topsides double-planked with ⅞-inch Douglas-fir over ⅞-inch cypress. Steel screws were used originally to fasten the inner layer to the outer one, and an extensive network of diagonal steel strapping went from the sheer to a metal body strap that generally ran along the lower part of the hull just above the tops of the floor timbers.

The original plank-to-frame fastenings were #20 brass screws and ⁵⁄₁₆-inch brass annular-thread nails for the bottom planking, with #18 brass screws in the topsides. Keelbolts, located between the floor timbers, were 1-inch Tobin bronze hanger bolts with the nuts against the top of the wood plank keel and the lag-screw ends extending 9 inches into the top of the lead ballast keel. The floor timbers themselves were secured to the wood keel with steel bolts, whose heads in the middle

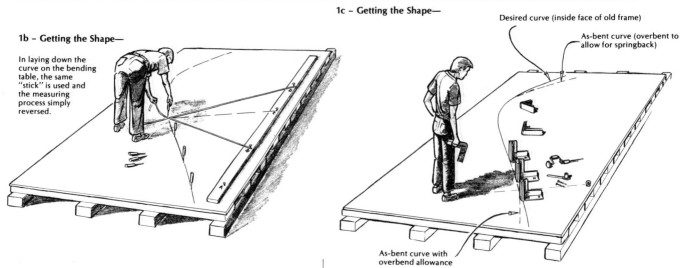

1b – Getting the Shape—

In laying down the curve on the bending table, the same "stick" is used and the measuring process simply reversed.

1c – Getting the Shape—

Desired curve (inside face of old frame)

As-bent curve (overbent to allow for springback)

As-bent curve with overbend allowance

part of the boat were sandwiched between the wood keel and the lead ballast.

By 1980, *Spartan*, one of two surviving New York 50s, was getting tired, even though she had had extensive work done to her in the late 1960s on the West Coast: laminated oak replacement and sister frames, lots of new stainless-steel fastenings, plywood ceiling and a new interior, and Dynel polyester sheathing over the entire outside of the hull. By the early 1970s, *Spartan* was in the Caribbean in the charter business. In 1974 her original pine deck was given a plywood and fiberglass overlay, and she received internal stainless-steel bracing and a new electrical system. Allen Pease purchased the yacht in 1978; he brought her north in 1980 and had her hauled that fall at Pilot's Point Marina in Westbrook, Connecticut, for "repairs."

As with most projects of this type, the extent of *Spartan*'s problems didn't become evident until she was opened up. Both the renewed frames from the 1960s and what was left of her original ones were in poor condition, her floor timbers and the bolts that secured them were badly deteriorated, and her planking, already suffering from many haphazard repairs and much refastening, had decayed under the Dynel skin. Most of the stainless-steel screws and bolts from her previous rebuild were in bad shape from crevice corrosion. It became evident to Mr. Pease that a quick repair job was not the answer.

Spartan was in tough condition, but she still had shape; the sheer was still fair, and measurements indicated that it was close to its original curve. There were no serious hard spots or unfairnesses in the hull, either, which was a testament to good structural design and to the ability of double planking to hold a hull in shape even after the frames had deteriorated. These factors were important in assessing the practicality of a major rebuilding.

Deciding what to do in a case like this isn't easy for an owner whose finances don't permit a boat to be rebuilt in one continuous operation. There's a temptation to throw the boat together quickly, go

sailing, and worry about the consequences later. Fortunately for *Spartan*, however, her owner is a farsighted individual; he decided to begin a complete rebuild with the understanding that the job could only proceed as fast as the money became available — and that would be slowly. While this isn't the most convenient arrangement for the people doing the work, and the overhead costs tend to take up a lot of the budget, it's still better in the long run than ruining the boat by doing a cheap or incomplete job.

With an owner steadily working to provide financing, and a cooperative and understanding boatyard management, the project proceeded slowly, but without any corners being cut.

My partner, Ben Philbrick, and I began work on *Spartan* in August, 1981. The hull had already been stripped of its ceiling and joinerwork, so we began by tearing out all the sister frames and extraneous material from inside the boat. We then made patterns of all the floor timbers — they all needed replacing — and prefabricated the pieces for new ones. We next removed and renewed about half these original floor timbers, temporarily fastening the original planking to them to help hold the hull in shape during the upcoming reframing. The planking was left intact during the framing process, though we removed one garboard for access. New frames were steam-bent outside the boat on forms, then installed, the other half of the floor timbers going in along with their corresponding frames. Along the way we replaced a section of the horn timber at the hole for the rudder stock, made and installed a new sternpost, added a reinforcing apron to the forefoot in the way of the maststep and the forefoot-keel joint, and replaced some of the deadwood.

Here's how we got out, bent, and installed the new frames:

Taking the Shape and Calculating for Overbend

The shape was taken off for every third frame. Measurements were made before the old frame was

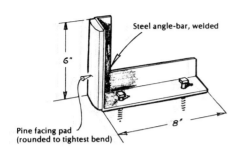

Steel angle-bar, welded

6"

Pine facing pad
(rounded to tightest bend)

8"

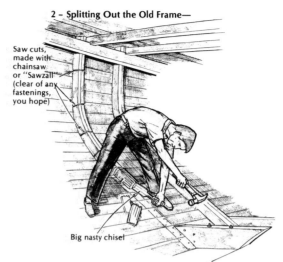

Saw cuts,
made with
chainsaw
or "Sawzall"
(clear of any
fastenings,
you hope)

Big nasty chisel

removed from the boat — to the inside face of the frame and far enough from the side facing amidships to get away from the partial bevel dubbed for the ceiling.

We took our measurements with a stick that was about 6 inches wide and approximately as thick as the ceiling bevel. A number of finish nails were driven into the stick, their positions identified by letters. The stick was clamped to the frame side of the deckbeam and the floor timber faces. Points were arbitrarily marked on the frame face and numbered for reference; they were approximately 1 inch apart — a little closer in tight curves, a little farther apart on flat runs. Using a cloth dressmaker's tape with a grommet near the end, which could be slipped over the finish nails, we made measurements from two or three different nails to each point marked on the frame. A table was kept of these measurements.

The nails were on the side of the stick away from the floor timber and the deckbeam to allow measurement into the bilge. The thickness of the stick made up for the ceiling bevel.

The curve of the inside of the frame was then duplicated outside the boat on the bending table by nailing the stick down and by crossing two tapes on two separate nails to reestablish each point on the curve. The top measurement was usually taken to a point under the sheer clamp, rather than at the frame head, since the clamp interferes with getting two measurements to the top. The top of the frame was then extrapolated with a batten when the points were faired in to establish the curve.

Once the curve on the inside edge of the frame was drawn on the table, the curve was analyzed and a new curve was established. This incorporated the correct amount of overbend at each point to allow the frame to fit well after it had cooled off and sprung back.

Predicting and allowing for the springback of a frame is necessitated by the large size of the boat and by the reframing method used. When replacement frames are small enough to be bent directly into the hull against the planking, a springback allowance is unnecessary, since the frames are held by C-clamps or fastenings and can't change their shape. Even if small frames have to be bent on a form outside the boat, the springback can usually be overcome just by pushing a little harder when

they are installed. *Spartan*'s big frames, 3-inches square, couldn't be manhandled as easily. It was best to overbend them, so when they were cool and were unclamped from the bending form, they would spring back to the desired curve. The technique for figuring overbend is quite involved; I'll summarize it here and let the accompanying chart provide more particulars.

Once the desired curve is laid down on the bending table, I divide the length into segments — usually 1-foot segments for a boat this size — over which the curvature can be assumed constant. The radius of curvature is determined for each segment, and then using a method based both on mathematical theory and empirical information, the required actual bending radius for each segment is calculated. From these calculated values, a new curve can be constructed that provides the proper amount of overbend.

This sounds complicated, but using a programmable calculator or the accompanying nomograph, it takes about 10 minutes to analyze a frame's shape and construct a new curve for it. We used the same physical and mathematical setup for bending three pairs of frames — the pair we actually measured for, and the pairs immediately forward and aft of it.

Setting Up the Form

The bending table itself is a heavy platform of 3-inch by 8-inch timbers with a plywood top measuring about 5-by 10-feet; it is cleated together underneath with 6 by 6s. The cleats used to bend the new frames against are of 3-inch by ¼-inch angle steel, welded together, with softwood pad facings, fastened to the form with ⅜-inch by 3½-inch lags. The bending cleats are high enough for two frames to be bent against them, one frame on top of the other.

Removing the Old Frames

The old frames were taken out by crosscutting every 6 inches or 8 inches with a Sawzall or Skilsaw at places where nails or screws were not likely to be lurking. (That's right, nails. *Spartan*'s original single

3 – Cutting the Bending Stock for Best Grain—

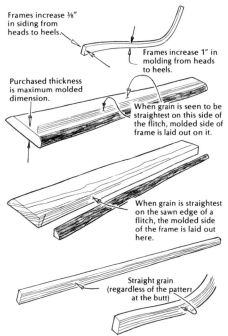

Frames increase ⅜"
in siding from
heads to heels.

Frames increase 1" in
molding from heads
to heels.

Purchased thickness
is maximum molded
dimension.

When grain is seen to be
straightest on this side of
the flitch, molded side of
frame is laid out on it.

When grain is straightest
on the sawn edge of a
flitch, the molded side
of the frame is laid out
here.

Straight grain
(regardless of the pattern
at the butt)

3a – Bending Frames—

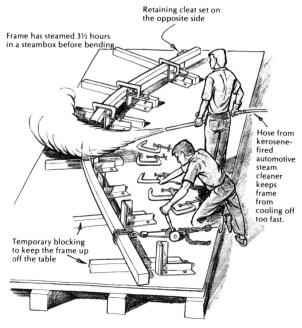

Retaining cleat set on
the opposite side

Frame has steamed 3½ hours
in a steambox before bending.

Hose from
kerosene-
fired
automotive
steam
cleaner
keeps
frame
from
cooling off
too fast.

Temporary blocking
to keep the frame up
off the table

planking was fastened with ⁵⁄₁₆-inch by 3½-inch brass ring nails into the frames and floors. Before they corroded away, they looked just like modern ring nails — annular grooves etc.) The pieces of frame were then split away with a big, nasty chisel, and the fastenings were pushed out through the planking. The diagonal strap grooves that had been cut in the planking were carefully cleaned out so new strapping could be fitted later.

Preparing the New Frames

The frames were 2½ inches square at their heads, increasing ⁵⁄₆₄ inch per foot to a maximum of 2⅞ inches in siding and a maximum of 3½ inches in molding. (We added three pairs of intermediate frames under the maststep; these were 2½ inches in siding all the way and a maximum of 2⅞ inches in molding.)

The frames were cut individually with a Skilsaw from white oak flitches; each cut was made carefully so the grain would run with the frame. I want to emphasize that the pore direction is the grain direction, regardless of the grain pattern on the cut surface. The grain pattern tells you something about how straight the grain will be on a side perpendicular to the one you're looking at and very little about the grain on the face where the pattern shows.

We purchased rough-sawn live-edge flitches that were as thick as the maximum molded dimension

Kerfed Frames—

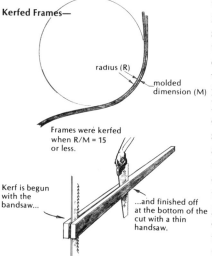

radius (R)

molded
dimension (M)

Frames were kerfed
when R/M = 15
or less.

Kerf is begun
with the
bandsaw...

...and finished off
at the bottom of the
cut with a thin
handsaw.

of *Spartan*'s frames. The stock was not run through a planer; blanks were cut right out of the rough-sawn flitches. We decided not to run our frame stock through a stationary thickness planer, because we have found it is more efficient to make both taper cuts with a bandsaw and finish off all four sides with a power-driven hand plane (a big, hungry Makita with carbide blades).

If we could see beforehand that the grain was straightest on the face of the flitch, the blank was sawn right out to the desired taper. If the grain ran straightest on the edge, the blank was sawn without taper to the proper 2⅞ inches siding. If we wanted to look at all sides before making a decision, we cut out a 3½-inch square blank and tapered it later after deciding on its best orientation. The taper in the molded dimension can sometimes be used to improve the straightness of the grain; conversely, if applied without care, the tapering can worsen the grain slope. Before steaming, the inside corners of each frame were rounded so we knew which way to make the bend.

All of *Spartan*'s original frames aft of amidships showed small tensile fractures along their convex edges. To prevent this type of failure in our new frames, we kerfed (slit) the sharply curving ones so they'd bend easier with less stress in the wood fibers. When a frame to be kerfed was tapered, an

Opposite frame of the pair
is bent atop the first.

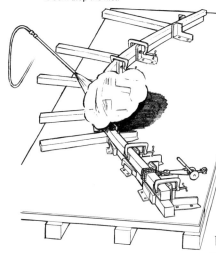

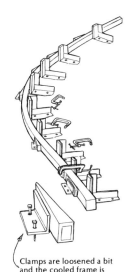

Clamps are loosened a bit
and the cooled frame is
slipped to the bottom of the
cleats and held there with
wedges. Clamps can then
be removed to make way
for the next frame.

allowance was made for the thickness of the saw cut so the finished molded dimension would be right. The kerf was cut on a bandsaw, except for the last 6 inches, which was cut by hand with a very thin saw so the kerf would close up wood-to-wood at the bottom. A Japanese ripsaw is excellent for finishing a kerf.

It pays to be very careful about selecting stock for frames of this size. We were looking for straight grain, especially for those sections of a frame at the sharpest bends. Each frame contained 10- to 12-board-feet of expensive wood that took quite a while to prepare; failures were too expensive to be tolerated. We ended up reframing almost the entire boat and only broke one frame in the process.

Straightness of grain on the convex and concave faces of a frame was not as critical as it was on the side faces. On the latter it was most important; straightness on the outer corner of this face was critical. The taper was laid out so the straightest grain ran along that corner at the tightest part of the bend. I disregarded entirely the way the annular rings ran on the ends of the frames in favor of getting the best grain along the side. If we couldn't get a grain slope better than 1 in 15 for a tight bend, we didn't bother to try bending the piece.

Steam-Bending the Frame

The frames were steamed for 3½ hours. The steam box temperature was carefully monitored with a meat thermometer with a mark at the boiling point. The temperature was not allowed to drop below 205 degrees F at the coldest part of the box except when water was added; it was maintained at 210 degrees F or above for the last 30 minutes

before the frames were bent. Proper temperature is very important — even a 5-degree difference can affect the ease of bending.

The steam box was fired with bottled gas; a kerosene-fueled automotive steam cleaner was used to assist during the actual bend.

The hot frame was taken from the box and clamped at its top end to the top cleat on the bending form. Reference marks on the form and the frame ensured proper positioning. If the curve were simple, an eyebolt was placed in an already drilled hole in the frame heel, beyond the point where the finished cut would be made. If the frame had a reverse curve, a strap was placed around the frame where the reverse occurred and a come-along was attached to it.

Steam from the nozzle of the steam cleaner was played on the frame to keep it limber while the come-along was slowly cranked up. The frame was clamped to each cleat as it came into contact. The frames were bent at the top of the cleats clear of the table to make any necessary twisting easier.

Once the first frame was bent, it was slid down to the bottom of the cleats — C-clamps still in place — and was wedged against short pieces of angle iron that were lagged flat to the table, allowing the C-clamps to be removed. The angle irons were positioned low enough to allow the second frame to pass over them and were situated between the cleats so as not to interfere with the clamps.

The kerfed frames were bent in the same way as the solid ones. However, instead of using a C-clamp at the top, another cleat was fastened at the outside of the curve; this allowed the inner and outer halves of the frame to slide past each other while the frame was being bent. When the bend was complete, a wedge was driven between this extra cleat and the frame head to force the head against the cleats on the concave side of the frame.

On simple curves, only a couple of angle irons were necessary at the bottom; on reverse curves, quite a few were necessary.

The frames, once bent, were covered with wet burlap to keep them from checking while they cooled. The next morning, stay laths were fastened to the frames, and the frames were removed from the form, beveled, and installed — usually all in the same day. The top stay lath was fastened on while the frame was still clamped to the cleats. Once removed, the frame was immediately turned over and its underside stayed. The lower frame was then slid up to the top of the form so a stay lath could be

3d – Bending Frames—

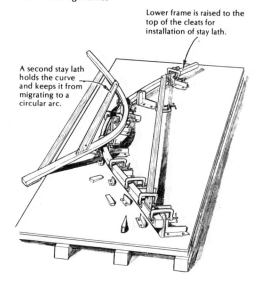

A second stay lath holds the curve and keeps it from migrating to a circular arc.

Lower frame is raised to the top of the cleats for installation of stay lath.

4a – Beveling the Frames; Picking Up the Bevels—

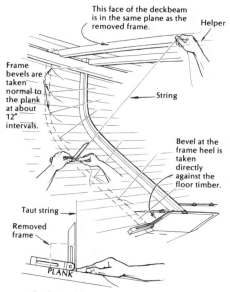

This face of the deckbeam is in the same plane as the removed frame.

Helper

Frame bevels are taken normal to the plank at about 12" intervals.

String

Bevel at the frame heel is taken directly against the floor timber.

Taut string

Removed frame

PLANK

fastened on while it, too, was still clamped to the cleats. No attempt was made to stay-lath the reverse curves at the heels of the frames. Because of widespread breakage in the old frames at this reverse, the frame heel areas were redesigned to ease the amount of curvature there. The new frames were allowed to run out fairly straight on the floor timbers and the resulting gaps were blocked out to the planking.

Kerfed frames were also allowed to cool overnight. The following day the two halves of the frame were fastened together with #12 screws spaced about 12 inches apart and driven from the concave side while the frame was still on the form. When released, the kerfed frame immediately sprang back a little (as allowed for when overbending), then held its shape and remained very stable without the use of stay laths.

Beveling

The bevels were taken from the boat and recorded for each frame, even though three or more frames were bent without resetting the forms. (For example, frames 17, 18, and 19 were bent on the form set up for frame 18.) We took the bevels at every foot along the frame line after the old frame was removed. One person held a sliding bevel against the planking, square against the frame line; the second person held a string against the deckbeam face or the opposite frame of the pair so the string ran along the blade of the sliding bevel. The bevel was adjusted to lie parallel to the string, and the angle, taken in degrees, was then recorded in a notebook. This method is more accurate than measuring against the side of the old frame before its removal.

The bevel at the frame heel was measured directly against the new floor timber, which was either temporarily or permanently in place, and also recorded in degrees.

The frame was then set up — with stay laths still on the unkerfed ones — on the bench. Using a table of calculated offsets for various bevels for a frame of 2⅞ inches siding, beveling points were marked off at every foot. The stay laths were located so they would not interfere with the beveling. The bevel offsets were interpolated by eye for the tapered top of the frame. All measurements were taken in ¹⁄₁₀₀ths of an inch.

The bevel marks were faired in by pencil and finger, guided by the convex corner of the frame. The frame was then beveled to this line with a power plane; a short power block plane was used in areas of reverse curve areas. Then the bevel was faired with hand tools and backed out slightly, so its outboard corners would make firm contact with the hull planking. (As Howard Davis always says, "Don't let it bind behind!")

Installation

Once beveled, a frame was hoisted into the boat, its head cut to fit against the covering board, and its inside face at the head dubbed a short distance for a good fit behind the clamp.

The length was measured with a fixed-length batten bent against the planking and pushed up against the covering board, and a measurement was taken from the end of this batten to the desired heel location. This length was transferred to the outer face of the frame, and the heel was cut, beveled, and limbered as necessary. The fit was then checked under the clamp, the stay laths removed, and the entire fit checked. If all was okay, the frame was taken out, coated with red lead primer on its top, bottom, and outside face and where it would lie against the floor timber, and put back into place for the final time.

Because all of *Spartan*'s hull planking was to be

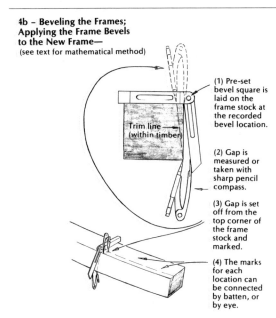

4b – Beveling the Frames; Applying the Frame Bevels to the New Frame—
(see text for mathematical method)

Trim line (within timber)

(1) Pre-set bevel square is laid on the frame stock at the recorded bevel location.

(2) Gap is measured or taken with sharp pencil compass.

(3) Gap is set off from the top corner of the frame stock and marked.

(4) The marks for each location can be connected by batten, or by eye.

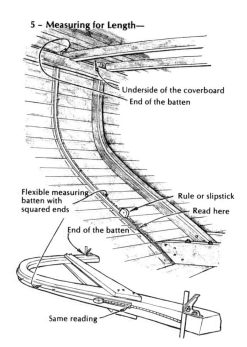

5 – Measuring for Length—

Underside of the coverboard
End of the batten

Flexible measuring batten with squared ends

Rule or slipstick
Read here

End of the batten

Same reading

6 – Installing the New Frame—

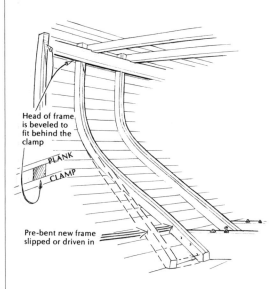

Head of frame is beveled to fit behind the clamp

PLANK
CLAMP

Pre-bent new frame slipped or driven in

7 – Bolting Frames to Floor Timbers—

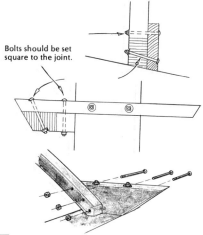

Bolts should be set square to the joint.

renewed eventually, the frame was only temporarily fastened at this time; #14 stainless-steel screws were driven through about every other plank. Before the lower end of the new frame was fastened into place, temporary fastenings were also driven from the planking into the new floor timber, as it is the floor timber and not the frame that establishes the shape of the hull in this area. The frame heel, clamped loosely to the floor timber, held the latter in vertical alignment while it was being attached to the hull.

Kerfed frames were beveled in the same way as the solid ones. A frame was brought into the boat, its top cut to the proper bevels, and after a test fit, coated with red lead. Then the upper, kerfed part of the frame was fastened into the boat with temporary #14 stainless-steel screws, which were not allowed to penetrate the kerf. Later, the permanent plank fastenings in the new planks would be driven across the kerf.

In the process of driving these temporary fastenings in a kerfed frame, or when the heel portion was being pulled in against the planking, it was likely that the kerf would tend to open up between the screws that held it shut. If this happened, the screws securing the kerf together were removed, and another set of screws was driven, starting from the bottom of the kerf and working up, until the kerf was tight again. The holes from the first round of kerf fastenings were then plugged. As a result of this adjustment, the inside part of the kerf would slide down slightly relative to the outside part, leaving it slightly shy of the covering board at the top. If the deck were off, this could be avoided by cutting the frame top flush after adjustment (it doesn't amount to very much — ¼ inch or ⅜ inch).

Once the planking was tight to the floor timber, the frame tight to the planking, and the floor timber tight against the frame, the permanent floor-to-frame bolts were installed. As with any fastening that must carry a shear load, these bolts must be installed square with the floor-to-frame faces in both directions.

Like *Spartan*, most older wooden boats, particularly if they have been refastened, will sooner or later be in need of complete or partial reframing. To people who haven't done much steam bending, the task often seems formidable. The work did on *Spartan* was, perhaps, a "worst case," few people will ever run into a bent frame task of this magnitude. But, as the foregoing indicates, even 3-inch-square oak can be dealt with successfully if you go about the job in the right away.

Calculating Overbend

OBJECT:

To find new chord-to-radius angles, so new points for the overbent frame can be laid out on the bending table.

PROCEDURE:

1. Divide the desired curve (the shape you want the inside edge of your new frame to be after it cools and springs back somewhat) into segments as shown. These segments should be short enough so the bend radius is essentially constant, yet long enough so there is enough chord height to measure with reasonable accuracy.

2. Measure the chord heights and lengths for each segment. You'll also need to know the molded dimension of the frame before you can use the nomograph.

3. For each segment, enter the nomograph at the bottom on the "chord height" scale. Extend the point vertically to the appropriate chord length curve, then move horizontally to the left to establish the bend's radius.

4. From the bend radius determined in Step 3 above, draw a straight line diagonally downward to intersect your frame's molded dimension on the scale entitled "frame molding."

5. From where the above line crosses the sloping straight line, you can determine the chord-to-radius angle for the overbent segment by extending horizontally to the right until you intersect the appropriate chord length line (one of the vertical lines at the right of the nomograph).

6. Go back to the bending table with chord-to-radius angles thus determined and plot these new angles for each segment, starting with any point on the original curve and using the same chord lengths as before. The result will be a series of points representing the overbent curve (see drawing). Fair them with a batten, if you wish, to see where the inside edge of the overbent curve should fall.

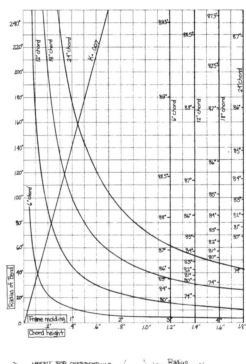

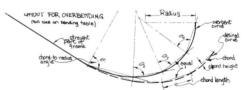

Stem, Transom, and Frame Repairs for a 12 ½ Footer

—— by Maynard Bray with photographs by Benjamin Mendlowitz ——

*I*n 1914 Nathanael G. Herreshoff created one of his best-loved designs, the Herreshoff 12½-footer, which he originally called the Buzzards Bay Boys Boat. Twenty boats of this new class were built that year; some 400 more were built by Herreshoff Manufacturing Company before production ceased in 1943. After World War II the Quincy Adams Yacht Yard built a few more under license from Herreshoff, followed by yet more from the Cape Cod Shipbuilding Co., which purchased all rights to this and several other Herreshoff designs in the late 1940s. Cape Cod soon ceased building 12½-footers in wood, turning to an updated fiberglass version they called the Bullseye. Then a few years ago Edey and Duff began building a fiberglass version of their own called the Doughdish.

Today, you can't buy a new, wooden-hulled Herreshoff 12½-footer, as Cape Cod Shipbuilding has retained all rights to both the design and its construction in wood. Many owners of existing 12½-footers wouldn't want a new boat, anyway; either they're too attached to the one that's been in the

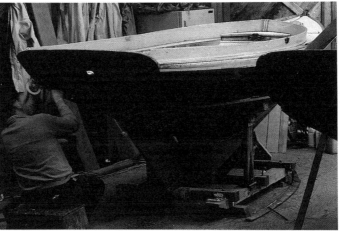

Although there are differences among boats, the first step in a total rebuild of a 12½-footer usually involves removing the deck, the transom, the stem, and two planks on each side of the boat — the garboard and another plank at the turn of the bilge. The boat shown is approaching that state; it has been blocked high off the floor for access and braced securely to hold her shape while rebuilding continues.

family for three or four generations, or if they didn't have one in the first place, they sought out an original that was up for sale and bought her. Keeping their old boats going is their main interest.

Wooden 12½-footers are showing their age almost without exception these days. Remember, all the Herreshoff-built boats are more than 50 years old, and most of the class are a good deal older than that. But these old hulls can, indeed, be given new life, although a good deal of skill is required for the job to be done well. The man who does this best and who has had far, far more experience at it than anyone is Steve Ballentine, whose yard in Cataumet, Massachusetts, on Cape Cod, has repaired some sixty 12½-footers; about 20 were total rebuilds. It's fussy work, and it isn't by any means cheap, but as Steve and his crew do it, the boats come out as strong as the day they were built, and they look just about the same as well.

Here is how Steve Ballentine repairs the stem, the transom, and the frames on a 12½-footer.

1

Steve has found over the years that the stems in these boats have held up quite well. Made of steam-bent oak, they rarely become rotten and generally require only refastening. But to refasten a stem properly, it must removed from the boat. Out on the bench, where it is accessible on all sides, the stem is cleaned up with a sharp scraper, particularly along the rabbet, where an accumulation of caulking and compound would interfere with refitting the planks. All the old screw holes are then filled with whittled oak plugs set in thickened epoxy, so the planking screws can be driven anywhere along it with the confidence that they'll hold. Similarly, the plank ends are cleaned up and their screw holes and damaged areas filled, this time with thickened epoxy alone. The stem is then ready for installation; new bolts are used at its lower end where it is scarfed against the keel. Plenty of bedding compound is applied to this joint before the stem is set in place, and a stopwater is bored for and driven in afterwards to keep it from leaking.

2

The use of thickened epoxy shows clearly in this photo. Epoxy gives the planking a new lease on life; it allows these full-length cedar planks, even though slightly damaged and worn, to be used again. For a good fit the second time around, some of the plank ends are dressed down with a block plane, as shown.

3

The story is quite different at the other end of the boat. If there is one thing that all 12½-footers generally need, it's a new transom. The originals were iron-drifted together, and their aft-raking inner faces made for easy entry of salt water. As always happens in a union of ferrous metal fastenings and seawater, rusting has sapped the strength from the drifts and caused the surrounding wood to go bad. Steve Ballentine corrects the immediate problem with a wholly new transom, and prevents a recurrence by using bronze rather than iron for the drifts and by backing up the strength of these fastenings with epoxy glue. The first step in this process is to carefully remove the old transom in one piece, so it can be used as a reference for making a duplicate. In this boat the vertical transom knee has been removed as well.

4

Oak ⅞ inch thick is used as stock for the new transom. The oak must be quite dry before assembly if the joints are not to open up afterwards. Here, Steve drives the bronze drifts, which will hold the transom planks together, into epoxy-coated holes. Wooden dowels are used in the middle and the ends to help with the alignment; metal has to be kept away from these areas so as not to risk damaging the edge tools that will later be used in cutting the finished shape of the transom and forming the hole for the tiller. (Since most of the lower piece will be cut away, no metal at all is used to fasten it — just glue. During gluing, this piece is held in alignment by a spline, which can be seen at the lower right in the photo.)

5

With the drifts driven half their length into one piece, the other (projecting) halves are coated with epoxy, as are the edges of both pieces of oak being joined. All the drifts have been carefully laid out to avoid conflict with any hardware that will later be attached to the transom, and the holes into which they are driven are sized for a fairly tight drive fit. Note that a blunt point has been ground on the end of each drift, so the fastening can be started more easily and can be driven without hanging up.

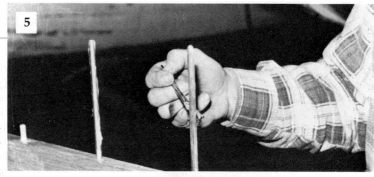

6

"Driving" is done by clamping one piece to another, as shown here. Steve is careful to bring the pieces together evenly so they don't bind. He measures frequently as he goes to ensure good alignment. He will also make sure that the pieces, once in contact and securely clamped, lie in a flat plane. One more piece, also drifted and glued, will be added after this one to provide the required width as indicated by the transom pattern, which can be seen standing against the bench in the background.

7

With the glue cured on all four pieces making up the transom, the clamps can be removed and a cutting outline can be marked in pencil from a master pattern that Steve has developed for these boats.

8

But not all 12½-footer transoms are exactly alike; differences from boat to boat show up when the old transom is laid on the master pattern. In most cases, the stripped-out hull can be pushed and pulled a little to conform to the pattern, since differences seldom amount more than ¼ inch.

9

With the old transom in place on the new material, common station marks are drawn about 2 inches apart and numbered as reference locations for lifting and marking the proper bevels along the edges of the new transom. The slight difference in outline between the old transom and the master pattern shows up here.

— 37 —

10
Bevels are now picked up very carefully from the old transom at each of the marked stations. This can be done in a number of ways; the method Dexter Cooper is using here involves marking the difference between the inner and outer transom faces on a piece of masking tape stuck to a small framing square.

11
This is the time to correct any gaps that may have existed between the transom and the hull planking before the old transom was removed from the boat. While the upper part of this transom appeared to fit well enough, it will be necessary to close up the gap or seam starting at station 7, as noted in pencil on the old transom before its removal.

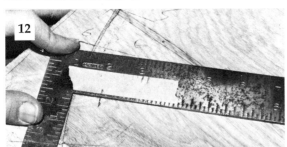

12
The mark on the tape is now transferred to the new transom. After all the stations have been so marked, the marks are connected with a fair line run through them.

13
The outermost of the two lines, representing the inner face of the transom, can then be sawn out and planed square, fair, and to the line.

14
Cutting the bevel, like marking for it, can be done in various ways. The idea is simply to remove the wood down to the marked line as quickly as possible, yet maintain the necessary control for a good job. Here, the bevel is being cut in several steps, the first of which is to make close-together saw cuts as shown, with the saw held so it hits the line at the same time as it hits the lower corner. A bevel gauge is used at this point and again on the finished transom edge to confirm that the bevel matches the old transom, except where deliberate departures have been made.

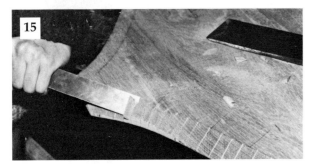

15
With a slick, a chisel, and, later, a spokeshave and a block plane, the wood between the saw cuts is removed and the beveled edge trued up.

16

The partially finished transom is ready for a trial fitting.

17

All the careful measuring and cutting has paid off. After the hull planking has been pulled into place against the new transom and held there with straps, braces, and clamps, very little trimming is required. At this stage, before fastening, the transom has to be held aft with a block of wood clamped to the keel at the bottom, and with wedges against the sheer clamps at the top.

18

So the few high spots can be planed off for a perfect fit, the transom is removed and clamped to the bench. Because the transom will be finished bright, this is also a good time to give the surfaces a final smoothing. After that, the surfaces must be protected against scratches and dents; here, Steve uses a blanket pad for that purpose.

19

Screw holes in the planking aft, as at the forward end of the boat, have been filled with thickened epoxy, so new holes may be drilled in optimum locations. The varnished sheerstrake, however, is an exception; old screw holes there are reused so as not to change the finished appearance. Before any drilling or fastening is done, the planks are wedged as necessary to create seams of even width.

20

Fastening can now proceed, with care taken to drill at the proper angle so the screws will get a good grip and not poke through the transom's inner face.

21

Here's the new transom, after the plank ends have been planed flush and the top of the transom has been shaped to the right curve. The hole for the tiller has yet to be cut. A new centerline knee (not visible) has also been made up and fastened to the inside face of the transom and the top of the keel. Now that the knee is in, the sternpost that covers its through-bolt at the keel can be installed. Actually, far more has been accomplished here than putting in the transom: the fin outside the keel timber has been rebedded and rebolted, some new planking has been hung, the sheer area has been rebuilt, and the boat has been completely reframed. The photos that follow show how the latter was done.

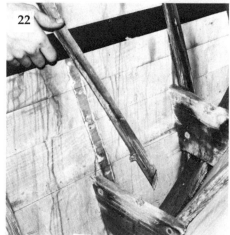

22

Steve has found that most old 12½-footers require new frames. Even though they look good on the three surfaces normally visible, the face against the planking, when revealed, usually shows signs of fatigue. The plank fastenings always need renewal, yet they're too weak to be backed out without breaking. New screws can be added, but drilling for them will take yet more strength from the already aged frames. More importantly, the planking will be weakened by the boring for additional screws. Thus, replacing the frames seems to be the best course of action. To do this, every other frame is removed in whatever way is quickest without damaging the rest of the boat. A hacksaw is sometimes useful here to cut off old fastenings, but splitting out the frames usually has to be resorted to. The remains of the screws are then driven out of the planking, using a hammer on the inside and a softwood backup block on the outside to avoid damaging the soft cedar. The putty over the screw heads has to be dug out first, of course; afterwards, the holes will be filled with thickened epoxy.

23

New frames of straight-grained oak are gotten out. Each must measure close to the correct length, with an extra allowance of 6 inches, and must be cut at the heel with the correct bevel. Each is tagged for location before being put in the steam box. After steaming for a half-hour or so, the frames are taken one at a time out of the steam box and quickly handed up into the boat.

24

Here's what the overall job looks like so far. You can see that the

way has been cleared for every other frame, and the planking in these areas has been cleaned of old paint and coated with linseed oil. The sheer clamp has also been wedged away from the remaining old frames so the new frames can be slid up behind it. The new transom and the two bulkheads, one forward (not shown) and one aft, help hold the hull in shape while the new frames are being bent in. The garboards and a plank at the turn of the bilge have been removed, which allows C-clamps to be used to draw the new frames into position. Here, Robert Williams limbers up a hot frame fresh from the steam box into the approximate shape it will have to assume when in place.

25
Pre-bending frames involves ingenuity. This frame must take an "S" shape; it is being formed by bending it over one knee and under the other, with the hands helping with the bend at the ends. The idea is to create a bend that is always fair and gradual; never allow the piece to bend sharply at one spot. That's how frames are broken.

26
Installation of a bent frame takes place in seconds — it has to because the wood is only flexible while it's hot. A frame out of the steam box cools quickly at room temperature. The first move after pre-bending is to drive the top up behind the sheer clamp, all the while trying to retain the pre-bent shape. This takes practice, but it's really easier than it sounds.

27
The first clamp is placed at the lower end of the frame near where it bears against the keel. This is where the reverse bend is located. To achieve the proper amount of curve in the frame at this point, a full-length ribband has been temporarily fastened about halfway up in the opening where the new garboard will go.

28
Once the heel is clamped to a good fit, the frame can be drawn out against the hull planking at the bilge with another clamp. Pads are placed under all the C-clamps, so the frames will not be marred when the clamps are drawn up tightly. Care should be taken to ensure that the planking pulls the frame toward it, rather than vice versa; this will maintain fair plank lines.

29
Although the hull has been stripped of paint, there is enough coloration on it to indicate clearly where the old frame landed and where the new frame must therefore go. This frame line sometimes needs improvement — each frame should be properly aligned to those adjacent to it. A rawhide mallet is used to tunk the frame whichever way is needed for alignment. After the first batch of frames is in place and fastened, the alternate frames will be split out, the surrounding planking stripped of paint, and the screw holes filled with epoxy to make way for new frames.

30

This is what the finished framing job looks like. This boat has also been given new floor timbers and new sheer clamps. With these additional members, the hull had enough stiffness so the bulkheads could be removed. The floors and the clamps were originally fastened with copper rivets, and those are what Steve has used in the new work. He has also decided to use rivets for the new plank-to-frame fastenings, rather than the flathead screws that had to be used when the boat was built. (There was a mold for every frame when all Herreshoff boats were built; the presence of these molds made riveting impossible.) Let's look at how the rivets were put in.

31

As mentioned earlier, all the old screw holes in the planking were filled with epoxy thickened with microballoons. From the inside face of the frame, pilot holes for each rivet were drilled all the way through the hull. The point of the twist drill shows in this picture, just emerging from the upper part of the lower plank. Rivet heads must be countersunk; a spade drill, centered in the pilot hole on the outside of the planking, does this job.

32

Copper rivets are driven through each of the holes; most planks having three rivets per crossing. A nail set is used to drive them all the way into their counterbores. Although it's doubtful there would be leakage around the rivets, just to be on the safe side Dexter wraps a strand of caulking cotton around the shank of each rivet, just under the head. The cotton is held in place with sticky bedding compound.

33

Now for the burrs, or roves, as they're sometimes called. These are a force fit over the rivet shanks; a short length of round bar with a hole drilled along its axis serves as a tool for driving them on.

34

The burr-driving tool is used with a hammer on the inside of the boat, while a helper bucks up the head of the rivet on the outside with a special iron (see photo 37).

35

End-nippers are used to cut off the excess length of shank, leaving just enough for peening. Usually an excess length equal to about the diameter of the shank is enough.

36

Peening is the next step. A light ball-peen hammer is used to tap lightly many times; this upsets the projecting end of the shank and forms it over the burr. Hard blows risk bending the shank inside the wood.

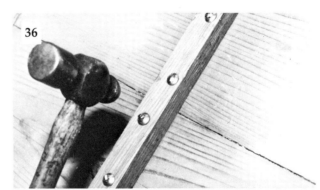

37

As when setting the burr, a bucking iron must held against the rivet head on the outside of the planking while the projecting end of the shank is peened. The tool for the job is a heavy iron weight whose end has been shaped to fit into the counterbore and against the rivet head. Steve uses a wooden block on this bucking iron to keep it from sinking the rivet head too deeply in the soft cedar.

38

Since the peened-over ends of the rivets will show on the inside of the hull, Steve dresses up their appearance with this tool. It smooths out the surface after peening and gives the rivets a more finished look. Outboard bucking is also required while this tool is used.

Extending the Life of a St. Lawrence Skiff

by Keith Quarrier with drawings by Kathy Bray

There are few St. Lawrence skiffs to be found in use today compared to the probable thousands that existed at the turn of the century. It's distressing to hear of those whose age has finally caught up with them. I heard of one fellow with a 70-year-old skiff who was going to plant flowers in it. I got there just in time to rescue her, though at that point she only had a duck decoy secured to the midship seat. The owner was about to drill holes in the bottom so rainwater would drain out. Luckily, I found that his "rotten antique" was basically sound, needing only to be refastened.

On another occasion, my aunt mentioned that her 50-year-old St. Lawrence skiff had reached the stage where it was "solely good for holding water." I jumped at the chance to look at this 18-foot lapstrake double-ender. She was framed with 46 white-oak ribs and was planked with northern white cedar. The keel and stems were also of white oak. Planking was lapstrake and fastened to the frames with clenched copper nails. I carefully removed some of the floorboards — they were not screwed but nailed to the frames — and found that all but five frames were rotten at the keel. The center sections of many of the frames were missing. I figured this was what made her leak; the planks were working from the lack of support.

"No problem," I told my aunt. "I'll take the boat to my shop in New Hampshire, and you'll be rowing among the lily pads next summer."

Preparations

In my shop, I removed the remaining floorboards. After labeling them, I wrote down their positions, because there wouldn't be a trace of where they had been fastened once the old frames were removed. Before removing the seats, I fastened an oak batten across the boat at the middle seat location, from gunwale to gunwale, to keep her from spreading at that point.

I have found that when "messing about" in old boats, it is impossible to know exactly what I will be getting into until all the problem areas have been completely surveyed. In this case, I thought that the framing was the only problem, but while probing around, I found that the keel was soft enough in a couple of spots to let in water; each spot was 6 or 7 inches long, by 1 inch wide.

The Keel

I decided to tackle the keel first, so I turned the skiff bottom up. With a set of chisels, I cut out the soft areas, leaving a smooth, beveled surface. I shaped so-called "dutchmen" of white oak to fit with a sabre saw and chisel. When a good fit was achieved, I glued the dutchmen in place with T-88 epoxy and weighted them down until the epoxy was dry. (Later, when the skiff was right side up, I applied more epoxy to the inside of the dutchmen.)

While working on the keel, I noticed that it was severely worn, so much so that when the boat was pulled up on a ramp, the garboard planks were taking some of the wear. I felt this had to be stopped and that a full-length keel band from stem to stem was necessary to protect the planking and to strengthen the weakened keel. The keel band was made of ½-inch-thick by 1½-inch-wide white oak, fastened with screws and epoxy.

Rot was found in some of the frames at the keel after the floorboards were removed. Before the seats were removed a single oak batten was fastened from gunwale to gunwale to help hold the boat's shape.

Because the original keel had been worn flush with the garboards, a shoe was added to prevent the further wearing of the garboards themselves.

Plank Fractures

While peering along my new keel band to make sure it wasn't cockeyed, I noticed half a dozen hairline cracks in the planking, 3 inches to 8 inches long, on each side of the boat. As I didn't want to get involved in replacing planks, I decided to make repairs by splining each of the cracks. By slightly widening each fracture with a linoleum knife, I found that by working slowly and carefully, a sliver could be removed without cracking the plank further. I spent a lot of time making sure that the inner edges were finished smoothly. Some new cedar shingles were at hand, and with a knife and a plane, I made splines from them to fit each crack, their grain running in the same direction as that of the planking. Once fitted, each spline was coated with epoxy and lightly tapped into place with a leather mallet. When the glue cured, I planed the splines flush with the outside planking. This may have been an unorthodox method of repair, but after two seasons these splines are watertight and still going strong.

The Frames

Forty-one of the 46 original oak frames and 34 sister frames were rotten at the keel; in fact, many of the frames were nonexistent at this point. I didn't want to sister-frame the skiff a second time for a number of reasons. First, additional frames would make the boat heavier; second, more fastening holes through the hull would be required, and I didn't want that; and third, I preferred to restore the skiff to a more original state.

I removed the old frames by splitting them from heel to head with a chisel, thus freeing the old fastenings. I didn't take out all the old frames at once, because I didn't want the boat to lose its shape. Pushing, pulling, and rocking is almost unavoidable when removing and adding new frames, so I felt the more support left in the boat the better. I removed only six old frames at a time before adding new ones.

I found it convenient to scrape and sand the old cracked paint on the inner surface of the planks before each set of new frames was put in place. Each new frame was made from a single piece of ⁵⁄₁₆-inch by ¾-inch white oak, just like the old ones. I bought a plank of white oak and had it planed to ¾ inch, the width of the frames, then I ripped it into ⁵⁄₁₆-inch strips on a friend's table saw. For a finished look, I shaved off a sliver on what would become the inboard facing edges with a hand plane.

Hot-Water Soaking
The oak I used was dry and wouldn't stand up to bending without boiling or steaming. My steam box

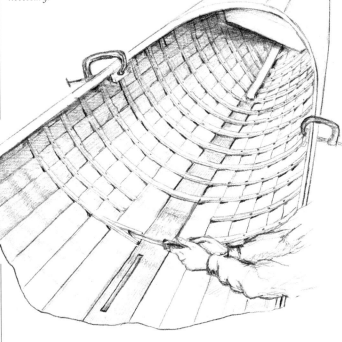

Old frames were removed by splitting them out, six at a time, with a chisel. New frames were clamped in place at the gunwales only, allowing them to be fitted tightly but shifted easily, if necessary.

was a 6-foot length of 1 ½-inch copper pipe with a cap brazed on one end, and was large enough for two frames to be boiled at the same time. At first, I poured boiling water into the pipe and then kept it at a boil with an ordinary propane torch, but later I discovered that it was unnecessary to use the torch; the hot water by itself was enough to soften the frames after a 20-minute soak.

While one pair of frames soaked, I fastened another pair into the skiff. The frames at the bow and stern were the most difficult to force into place without cracking because of their sharp turn across the keel. After numerous failures, I found that by boiling each of these frames a bit longer than the rest, and by coating them with linseed oil beforehand, they became pliable enough to bend without cracking.

Fitting and Fastening
In order to fit each frame snugly against the planks to make fastening easier, I clamped each end of the frame at the gunwales, loosely enough to allow me to push the frame downward so it would make contact with the planks, yet tightly enough so that it couldn't spring upward again. When clamping, I lined up the frame so it covered the old fastening holes in the planking. Beginning with the garboard plank on either side and working

A small pocket of rot had developed in the keel, so a dutchman was fitted and glued in place. The rotten wood was cut neatly away, leaving a rectangular recess beveled on four sides to accommodate the bevels of the dutchman.

upwards to the gunwale, I drilled from the outside, through the old hole, into and through the frame.

For fastenings, I used copper clench nails. Before driving each nail in place, I applied bedding com-

Hairline cracks in the planking were repaired by cutting-in straight recesses and gluing beveled splines in place.

pound to the head. With light blows, I drove in the nail and then clenched it while holding a heavy hammer as a bucking iron on the head. I screwed each frame to the keel, as I felt nails wouldn't hold well enough in the age-softened keel. I then filled the holes in the planking for the old sister frames with cedar plugs set in epoxy.

Ordinary woodworking tools worked fine for the entire repair job, except for the planing and ripping of the oak frames; the thickness planer and table saw needed for these operations can be rented or borrowed.

If you have ever compared the rowing qualities of an original St. Lawrence skiff to a fiberglass reproduction, you know it's worth the effort to keep your antique skiff in rowing condition. With a little time, effort, and ingenuity, many antique skiffs can be repaired. After all, skiffs are only as old as they feel.

Removing Tension in New Frames

— by Ulf Henrikson with photographs by Janicke Henrikson —

While rebuilding a 1906 vintage motor launch here in Sweden, I found the heavy pine planking in remarkably sound condition, but the oak keel, stems, and frames were all in an advanced state of deterioration. The boat is similar to the Fay & Bowen type of launch and measures 25 feet 3 inches by 5 feet 3 inches.

I replaced the keel, the floors, and the stems, and began work on the frames. I removed the old frames, every second pair at a time, steamed new 1-inch by ¾-inch ones, bent them into place, and copper riveted them in the normal manner. All but the 10 most forward frames were replaced — there were 68 in all. In the process, the boat grew some 5¼ inches wider than she had been before.

Keep the Shape

I was not totally ignorant about the importance of keeping the boat's shape while reframing her. I had used different types of support while disassembling the hull, but my efforts in that direction were apparently not quite good enough. The covering board and coaming could not cope with the tension produced by the new frames; the problem caused me a number of sleepless nights while I tried to figure out a solution.

The main task was to get rid of the tension in the frames, but first I had to pull or push the sides inward, back to the shape they should have. I could not simply tie the sides together, because that would inevitably result in an uneven hull.

Luckily, the construction of this particular boat included an engine bed, which also acted as stringers, stiffening the hull. This was the ideal member to pull the sides in against. I used steel bands, the type used to hold loads on a pallet. They have the advantage of being absolutely stiff, and the tool needed to tighten them allows you to be very accurate. A string tied from stem to stern down the centerline served as a reference point, and I was able to bring the hull back to her former shape.

Solving the Problem

I still had to face the problem of removing tension from the new frames. If I could have steamed the entire hull, the problem would have been solved, but steam boxes of that size are somewhat scarce in this country. I decided to tackle the problem one bit at a time.

First I borrowed an electric hot-air blower from a company that installs plastic tubes for ventilation, etc. They use the blower to heat the tubes before bending them to shape; the same type of blower is often used for paint and varnish removal. This machine was equipped with a custom-made U-shaped nozzle that was suitable for the task at hand.

Next I tried the blower on a broken, rejected frame that had been steamed once. I wanted to determine whether an already steamed piece of wood could be reshaped once more, since this was what I had to do with the frames in the boat. I clamped the old frame over a block of wood and placed the blower over it, holding it for three or four minutes over every 5 inches. I had to turn the blower down from maximum heat effect (3,050 watts) to 80 percent to keep the wood from charring. The blower had five heat settings. After removing the clamps on the test piece, I discovered that the method worked.

The Job Accomplished

Turning now to the hull, I protected the planking with cardboard, splashed linseed oil on the first frame to be rebent to help distribute the heat, and went to work. I started where the floor ended and held the blower there for three minutes. The copper rivets in the frame carried the heat nicely right through it. I could see the oil boiling a couple of inches above the section where I was working. Obviously, the hot air raced up the frame and preheated it. Consequently, I found I could reduce the time I held the blower over a section as I moved up the frame. Each frame took about 10 minutes.

The whole job took 12 hours — 12 very boring hours — but the results were worth it. When I clipped the steel bands, the hull was only ½-inch wider than it should have been. I don't think any method could bring it much closer. Of course, I could have pulled the sides in a little farther with the steel bands, but it would have been difficult to determine just how much this should have been. It was simple to correct that ¼-inch deviation on each side when I fitted the new covering board.

Using a hot air blower proved to be a good method for easing the tension in the new frames so my boat would hold her shape. I'm sure it can be adapted to solve other kinds of problems as well.

The U-shaped fitting that came with this blower proved perfect for heating the frames.

The heat from the blower traveled quickly up the frames. About 10 minutes were required for each 1-inch by ¾ -inch frame

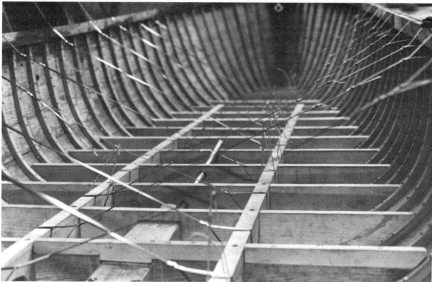

I used steel strapping to pull the hull into shape, and anchored the strapping to the engine-bed stringers.

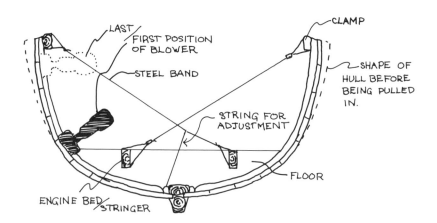

Making Laminated Frames

——— Text and illustrations by Arch Davis ———

*I*t's blowing a good Force 6, and you are driving your boat to windward as hard as she will go in open water. A gust hits just as a particularly large wave bears down; at full speed the boat bursts through the toppling crest, almost becoming airborne on the other side. You hang on as she crashes down in a storm of flying water, rigging quivering like harp strings, then grit your teeth as she staggers back to press on to meet the next assault.

This is the stuff of which leaking garboards and sprung seams are made. The stresses involved can be easily calculated. For example, the tension in the keelbolts can be obtained using a cross section, as in Figure 1. The situation is simplified by assuming that the boat has been knocked down to 90 degrees, and that there are 10 keelbolts on the centerline. Assume further that deceleration as the boat brings up in the trough is enough to give g=2, and the figures become somewhat intimidating.

In a modern wooden sailboat, laminated frames distribute these large stresses, and the corresponding stresses generated by the mast and rigging, into the hull. Such a boat can quite easily be made strong enough to be pushed to windward in heavy weather with no ill effects.

If you are building a keelboat of cold-molded construction, you will probably have a number of large, laminated frames to make. These can in some cases all be made beforehand. They can be set up along with any sawn or temporary frames that the design calls for, and the planking can be laid over them. Or some or all can be made to fit the planked hull and installed later. The techniques used in the latter case would also apply to a finished boat that showed signs of weakness in a high-stress area and required strengthening. Installing a set of laminated frames under the maststep, however, is a major undertaking that requires the removal of the cabin furniture in the area involved, but if planned as part of an extensive rebuilding program it may be a practical way of giving an aging hull a new lease on life.

In principle, making a set of laminated frames is simple. A number of strips of wood are spread with glue, clamped together to the right shape, then either planked over or dropped into an existing hull to be glued, screwed, bolted, riveted, or nailed in place. In practice there is much to think about, a lot of planning to be done, and not a few pitfalls to be avoided.

Preparing the Wood Stock

The design should specify the type and size of lumber you need. Obviously, the stock should be as straight and free from defects as possible. Inevitably, some pieces will not be quite straight, and since it is virtually impossible to apply edge-set at the same time as bending laminations around a tight curve, the stock will have to be somewhat wider than the finished frames. One-half to three-quarters of an inch is not too much to allow for a boat of moderate size.

Probably the lumber will have to be resawn. Some experimentation may be necessary to determine what finished thickness is best for the job. Thin laminations are easy to bend, but since there will be more of them, they will require more glue and more time to spread it — which can be an important consideration, as we shall see. Thinner laminations also require more clamps, more closely spaced. Since the waste produced in resawing each lamination is the same regardless of its thickness, thin laminations are more wasteful of lumber than thick ones, other things being equal. It will normally be necessary to allow ⅛ inch for the kerf of the saw, and at least another ⅛ inch for planing. Rough-

Figure 1

Simplified calculation for tension in keelbolts:
L.O.A. 40 feet. Displacement 10 tons. Ballast 4.5 tons.
10 keelbolts on centerline. Knocked down to 90°. g = 2.
Fulcrum F lower edge of lead ballast bearing on stub keel.
Weight of ballast x lever arm (C.G. ballast to F) x g equals
T x number of keelbolts x lever arm (keelbolt to F).
i.e. 10,080 x 1.06 x 2 = T x 10 x 0.29

$$T = \frac{10,080 \times 1.06 \times 2}{10 \times 0.29}$$

= 7, 369 lb
= 3.29 tons
i.e. each keelbolt subjects its floor to a stress of 3.29 tons.

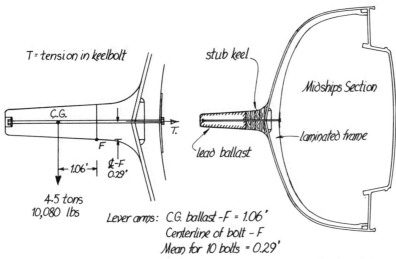

T = tension in keelbolt

C.G.

F

T.

stub keel

Midships Section

laminated frame

lead ballast

1.06'

ℓ-F 0.29'

4.5 tons 10,080 lbs

Lever arms: C.G. ballast -F = 1.06'
Centerline of bolt - F
Mean for 10 bolts = 0.29'

In most cases the situation will be more complex - some keelbolts will be paired and there will be correspondingly fewer floors or frames. Mean tension in paired bolts remains the same as above; floor is subject to twice the stress. Structures are subject to simultaneous forces in several directions, due to pitching, rolling etc.

Note that if the frame or floor is seen as a beam under a bending load, the total depth of the beam may be taken from the top of the frame to the to the outside of the planking in a boat of laminated construction where the planking provides strength under tension.

sawn stock 1 inch thick will yield two 5/16-inch laminations, or three at 5/32 inch. Thicker stock may be resawn economically to different thicknesses. Some juggling of sizes may help maximize the usable lumber you get from the available stock.

If you can, do the resawing and machining yourself. If you have to hire someone to do it, try to arrange to be present to "help" — really to keep an eye on things and make sure you get a good job. The average lumberyard employee is not much concerned with wasting your precious wood, and he may blithely push a number of laminations through the planer the same side up, and not even notice.

Bandsaws are best for resawing, but sometimes the blade bows in the cut, due to unequal set on the teeth, with consequent waste when the resulting curved surface has to be planed flat. If you have tried bending some laminations to the curves involved, you will know whether you can afford to go a hair over the specified thickness, and save one or two laminations in each frame, or whether it would be better to make the laminations slightly thinner, if this means you can squeeze one more from each piece of stock. Only you can make these decisions — even an experienced and helpful wood machinist can only do what you decide is best.

Make sure you have enough lumber of sufficient length. A frame running gunwale-to-gunwale in a 30-footer with a 10-foot beam may require stock 16 to 18 feet long.

Preparing to Bend

If you are making frames prior to planking the hull, their shape will be taken from the lofting floor. The section at the frame position is found, the thickness of the planking and other members, such as the keelson or stringers, is deducted, and a curve drawn, giving the shape of the outside of the frame. If you are not concerned about damage to the lofting surface, the frame can be glued up right there, on the line. One way would be to use a set of welded steel dogs (Figure 2), fixed at strategic points along the curve with lag screws. It is a simple matter to move the dogs for each frame. Obviously, you won't do this if your workshop has a good planked floor that you don't want to mar with screw holes, but if the sections were lofted on ¾-inch plywood, that surface will have enough thickness to hold the dogs against the considerable clamping stresses. (The damage to the plywood is less than you might expect, and it may well be useful later in building, with the worst areas cut out.)

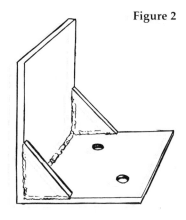

Figure 2

If the frames are being fitted to an existing hull, you will need some type of jig or mold. This could be a set of dogs on a sheet of plywood, or an arrangement made from scrap lumber, as shown in Figure 3. Whatever it is, it will have to be strong enough to withstand the forces produced when you wind the clamps to pull all the laminations together. The shape will be taken in this case from a pattern made to fit inside the hull where the frame will go.

Some time before gluing up the first frame, a good deal of sorting through your lumber will be necessary. It probably came out of the planer in an assortment of lengths; some pieces may be less than straight on edge, and there may be defects such as knots or short grain. Wherever possible, cut out defects. Even if you are making "ring" frames measuring 16 feet from gunwale-to-gunwale, these will probably taper in thickness at the ends, so you will need some shorter pieces. Badly curved pieces may best be used by cutting them into shorter lengths.

If your lumber has some defects that you cannot avoid using, all is not lost. From a mechanical standpoint, a frame may be treated as a beam that will be subjected to bending stresses. The stiffness of the beam is the main concern. When a beam is subjected to a bending load, stresses are set up in the beam. These are oriented along the beam; compression stresses develop on the edge where the load is applied, and tension stresses develop on the opposite edge. These stresses are greatest at the surface, diminish toward the middle of the beam, and become zero at what is called the neutral axis. The entire beam, including the middle part, is subject to shear stresses; the layers of the beam try to slide lengthwise on one another (Figure 4). A knot, or short grain, which would be weak in tension, but which would not much affect shear strength, will have least

effect on the strength of the beam if it is located in the middle.

The moral? Keep your best, cleanest lumber for the outside surfaces of the frame. If you have to use a less-than-perfect lamination, put it in the middle of the frame.

Unless the backyard builder is particularly well equipped, finding enough clamps for a large laminating job is likely to be a problem. A big frame, with hard curves at the turn of the bilge, takes a lot of pulling into place. You will need plenty of heavy, powerful clamps. Life will be easier if some of them are of the sliding bar type. These are good at the initial stages of pulling the laminations into shape; the big ones open a long way, and you can push on the laminations and slide the clamp in as far as you can, where it will lock in place, without winding on the screw. A jig of the type shown in Figure 3 has the advantage that it allows the use of clamps made from carriage bolts and two pieces of 2-by-4 lumber. These are slower to do up than a C-clamp, but they are cheap and simple to make, and they apply even pressure across the width of the frame. With C-clamps, pads must be used. These should be long enough to span the width of the frame, and thick and stiff enough to apply pressure at the edges.

Figure 3

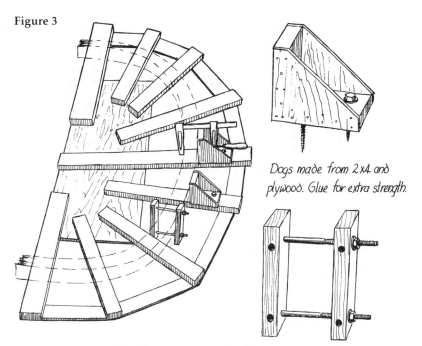

Dogs made from 2 x 4 and plywood. Glue for extra strength.

Jig made from ¾" plywood and 2"x6" and 2"x4" must be strong enough to resist deforming under load. Dogs are positioned using a pattern, and fixed with lag screws. Homemade clamps from 2 x 4 and carriage bolts may be used between arms of jig. Holes drilled both ways speed assembly with laminations of varying thickness.

A Dry Run

As for any but the simplest gluing job, a dry run is advisable before assembling the first frame. The pieces must be selected and stacked in order. They should be cut a little longer than the finished frame. It is helpful to straighten the down-side edges of curved laminations.

It may be possible to do some pre-finishing of the laminations before they are glued up. For example, if the frame tapers in thickness, you may want to round over the ends of the shorter laminations, and sand surfaces that will be exposed on the finished frame. This is easier to do now than it will be later on the concave inner surface of the finished frame. To keep track of the placement of these laminations, put a mark on the edge of each lamination, at the center.

Lay the stack of laminations on edge in the gluing jig, and pull them into shape with your clamps. A 6-inch-thick frame would contain 19 laminations ⁵⁄₁₆ inches thick. One piece may bend around the required curve quite easily; 19 together is another story. For a gunwale-to-gunwale frame, it is probably best to start by pushing the stack in at the enter; then, when this has gone as far as it seems to want to, start clamps at the turn of the bilge on each side. As the frame gets closer to the jig, start more clamps and pull in evenly over the entire length. This reduces the chances of breakage due to forcing too tight a bend at any single point. The best method will depend on the shape you have to achieve. As you tighten the clamps, push the laminations firmly down on the bottom of the jig, so that the edges are as even as possible.

When you are satisfied that you know how the wood will behave, where extra clamps are needed, where the frame wants to distort, and what to do about it, take the entire assembly apart. Lay out the clamps and pads so they will come readily to hand on the final assembly run. Stack the laminations in order, ready for spreading the glue.

Laminating the Frame

On a large laminating job, one or two assistants are almost essential. You will be working to a time limit. The glue must be mixed and spread, the laminations laid in the jig, and all the clamps tightened before the first batch of glue has jelled to the extent that it will not readily squeeze out of the joint.

Care is needed in mixing large batches of epoxy, since the mixture will generate heat and may set up prematurely. One-gallon plastic ice cream containers are good for mixing larger batches of epoxy, as they allow thorough mixing of resin and hardener. To help prevent excessive heat buildup, the mixed glue can be spread up around the sides of the container somewhat, rather than being left in a single big dollop in the bottom, which concentrates the heat.

The spreading of epoxy thickened with cotton fiber and silica is best done with a toothed squeegee, though such a technique takes time. Unthickened epoxy resin may be spread with a roller, which is quicker, but it is very runny stuff; when you turn the laminations on edge to put them in the jig, the glue will immediately start to sag. This can be prevented by stretching plastic film over the jig. As the clamps are tightened, the laminations should

Figure 4

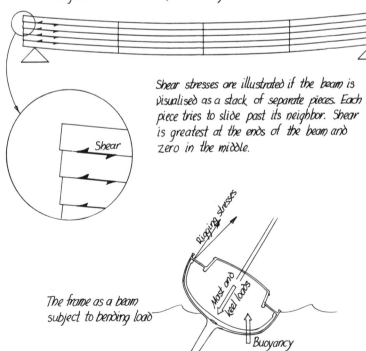

Under a bending load, the top of the beam is shortened, while the bottom edge is stretched, setting up compression and tension stresses. These are greatest at the surface, diminishing to zero at the neutral axis.

Shear stresses are illustrated if the beam is visualised as a stack of separate pieces. Each piece tries to slide past its neighbor. Shear is greatest at the ends of the beam and zero in the middle.

The frame as a beam subject to bending load

Figure 5

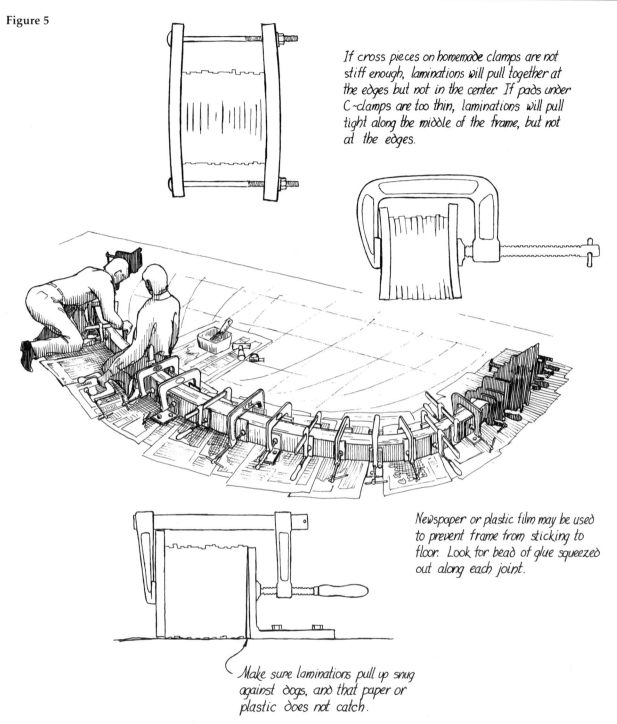

If cross pieces on homemade clamps are not stiff enough, laminations will pull together at the edges but not in the center. If pads under C-clamps are too thin, laminations will pull tight along the middle of the frame, but not at the edges.

Newspaper or plastic film may be used to prevent frame from sticking to floor. Look for bead of glue squeezed out along each joint.

Make sure laminations pull up snug against dogs, and that paper or plastic does not catch.

take up the pooled resin, which will be squeezed back into the joint. The plastic film must be stretched tightly so it cannot be caught between the laminations.

A roller can be used with resorcinal glue, if that is your choice. Resorcinal or epoxy — a roller with a built-in reservoir speeds the process.

Wear gloves. No matter how careful you are, you'll have glue up to your elbows before you know it. A good, strong pair of rubber gloves can be

reused many times. When you are done, allow the glue to set, stretch the gloves, and most of the hardened glue will loosen and fall off.

It may be best to apply glue to all the laminations, stack them up, and put them into the jig together. Alternatively, you may find it more convenient to put them in the jig one by one as they are buttered up, with some arrangement to hold them partly curved, ready for clamping. When applying the glue, start spreading on the outside lamination.

Figure 6

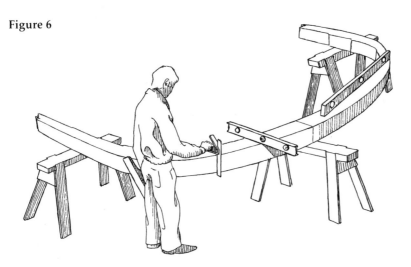

True the frame with levels and try square.

Then, if time runs out and the glue begins to harden, you can put the laminations you have ready into the jig and clamp them up. The other (inside) laminations can be added later.

However you proceed, you will need something — plastic, newspapers, scraps of wood — to prevent the frame from becoming glued to the jig. The advantage of wood scraps is they cannot get caught between laminations. They will stick, of course, but they are easily removed in the process of dressing the edge of the frame.

Now the fun begins. It may have seemed tricky enough pulling those laminations into shape on the dry run; it is much more difficult now. Fresh glue is slippery, and the laminations take the least opportunity to spring out of the jig. In particular, the ends will try to work up and slide over the jig. If this happens, the entire assembly is liable to fly apart in a sticky, maddening mess. Two assistants, firmly holding the ends of the frame down on the jig, will prevent such a disaster.

While the glue is still wet, the laminations will also try to slide past each other, so the marks in the centerline no longer line up. A good deal of cajoling will be necessary to correct this. Probably you can't get those marks exactly in line — but that's why you cut the laminations long in the first place.

Individual laminations will try to kick up at one end or the other. They must be firmly pushed back into place. Notwithstanding the need for speed, take your time. If you rush, something surely will go wrong.

What do you do if a lamination breaks at this point? There may simply not be time to take everything apart, cut and prepare a new lamination, apply glue to it, and assemble the frame again. If the break occurs near the middle of the frame — which is likely, as that's where you put laminations

that looked the least bit suspicious — fill the break with glue, push the laminations together, and clamp the assembly tightly. Such a repair on the fly will probably have no measurable effect on the strength of the finished frame.

At last, all the clamps are tight. There should be a bead of glue squeezed out along each joint between laminations. Look for gaps, where an extra clamp or two might be needed. Is the frame sitting squarely in the jig, or has it twisted somewhere? An extra clamp may be needed to snug it up tightly.

Notice that if the pads under your C-clamps are not long enough or not stiff enough, the laminations will be pulled together in the middle, but not at the edges; conversely, with a homemade clamp of carriage bolts, if the wooden cross pieces are not stiff enough, the laminations will squeeze up at the edges but not in the middle (see Figure 5). When you are satisfied, wipe off as much excess glue as you can, clean up the area, peel off your gloves, and take a break. You probably need it.

Cleaning up the Frame

When the glue has set, take the frame out of the jig. Laminated members made from a small number of pieces may be subject to springback when the clamps are taken off, which should have been allowed for when the jig was set up. But in the type of work we are considering here, with perhaps eight or nine or more laminations, the piece will not spring back noticeably when removed from the jig. Even so, when the frame is offered up to the line on the lofting floor, or the pattern from the hull, it will probably be found to only approximate the shape required, and a good deal of work will remain.

Start by knocking off the larger excrescences of glue with a chisel, scraper, hatchet — whatever lies to hand — and set the frame on three sawhorses. Now you have to dress the edges of the frame to the required width, and make them smooth, parallel, and square to the outside face.

Several things may be immediately apparent. Unless your stock was somewhat wider than the frame was designed to be, the frame may end up undersized, as the edges of the laminations will be far from perfectly lined up, and you will have to take ¼ inch to ⅜ inch off each side to make them smooth. You may also notice that the frame is a little twisted where it was not pulled tightly against the jig, so the outside face is not quite perpendicular to the plane of the frame. (You are not worried about the inside face, since it doesn't have to fit anything in particular.) And you can't sight along the frame, because of its curvature — so how do you make sure the sides are true?

Start by hoeing into one side of the frame with a sharp power plane. Cut back the most obvious high spots; then, eyeballing the frame as you go, work on it until the side begins to approximate a reasonable state. Turn the frame over and do the other side.

Now use your level to true up one side. Place the level across the frame to ensure that the side will be perpendicular in the boat. Next place it along the frame, to ensure that the side lies in the plane of the section (see Figure 6). Continue using the power plane to clean up the side, then finish off with a No. 6 or 7 hand plane until all edges of the laminations are flush with each other and the level shows that the side is true. Turn the frame over and work on the other side, finishing the frame to the correct width. (The second side can be finished with a thickness planer, if you have one.)

Now the outside face of the frame must be finished. Eventually, the frame will have to be beveled to fit the boat, but for now it is helpful if the face is made square. This can be checked with a try-square from one of the now-true sides. The face must also be planed to fit the shape on the loft floor, or the pattern from the hull. This is a simple matter of marking and planing; an extra lamination may have to be added to part of the frame to fill it out if it is undersized. Pieces also may have to be added to accommodate the keelson and gunwales. Finally, the frame must also be cut to length.

If the frame is being made prior to setting up and planking the hull, there is little left to be done. A temporary cross-brace for setting up may be required, and the centerline should be accurately marked. Beveling the frame to take the planking will be left until all the frames are set up and the backbone of the boat is complete.

A frame made to go into an existing hull, however, must be pre- beveled. After the shape of one edge (the after edge of forward frames, and the forward edge of the after frames) has been established, a series of bevels may be taken from the hull, marked on the patterns, and transferred to the frame. Final fitting will require the frame to be taken into the boat and scribed against the hull.

Laminating in Place

Laminated frames may also be made inside an existing hull, without the need for patterns, jigs, and fitting. This works best when the frames are relatively small, without too much curve — for example, in the bottom of a boat with a chine. The main problem with this method is in finding fastenings with sufficient power to hold against the tendency of the laminations to pop out. In most cases, screws will be too slow to use and/or expensive,

and even ring nails will pull out if the load is too great. Thinner laminations may bend in more easily, but the number of fastenings involved may make their use unrealistic.

Another factor making lamination in place problematical is that dressing up the sides of the frame is difficult. Furthermore, the frame may not sit plumb. For example, a frame near the bow where there is a good deal of shape will cant aft at the top. This may not be a concern, or it may be overcome by using a first lamination with a wedge-shaped cross section.

XI

An Alternative Frame-Repair Technique

-------- by Daniel McNaughton --------

One of the more common ailments that old age or improper engineering can produce in a boat is broken frames. The cause could be over-steaming of the wood when the boat was built, excess flexibility of the hull, or stress concentrations in parts of the hull. Broken frames typically occur in any area of the hull that has curves of small radius; they are also common behind overly rigid bilge stringers.

Sister Frames

The most common traditional repair technique has been to "sister" the broken frame by laying in another partial frame next to it. The major disadvantages of this method are that it results in additional fastening holes, which weaken the planking, and it encourages a stress concentration in the sister, opposite the break in the original frame. In the latter situation, the sister is actually weaker than the original frame and will usually break at the stress point sometime in the future. Other disadvantages to sistering are that it does not truly restore the old frame to new condition, and it is pretty much a one-time repair. Combined with the tendency of the sister frame to break in a similar fashion to the original (in a shorter period of time), this means that a large-scale sistering job may put a practical limit on the life span of the boat, something which would not occur had the repair been done properly. What's more, as sister frames often look slipshod when exposed to view, potential buyers are often more turned off by them than they would be by unrepaired broken frames.

Traditional Frame Repair

"Proper" frame repair is difficult and time consuming. The traditional method is to pull off the covering boards, remove the old frame and its fastenings, and steam in a new frame in the old one's place. If the boat doesn't have covering boards, you have to cut away the edge of the deck for access. And it's often necessary to remove a large part of the interior of the boat in order to gain access to the frame along its entire length.

To avoid some of these difficulties, you can laminate replacement frames in place, snaking the veneers behind the clamp and the interior joinerwork. While the results can be beautiful and strong, the method is time consuming and expensive. And because a thin, flat piece of wood will not bend in both directions between its top and bottom ends (as a steam-bent frame will do), it's often impossible to reuse fastening holes; one of the advantages of frame replacement will be lost.

Healing the Break

After we gave these problems some thought and conducted some experiments, our professional boatyard has developed a method that makes "proper" frame repairs easier and faster. It's ideal for repairing "tension" breaks, where an otherwise perfectly good frame has a clean break, and it should be helpful in any instance where the hull planking is not out of alignment due to the frame problem.

Our method is similar to one described by Bud McIntosh for making quick and neat repairs to spars. It consists of "healing" the broken frame by

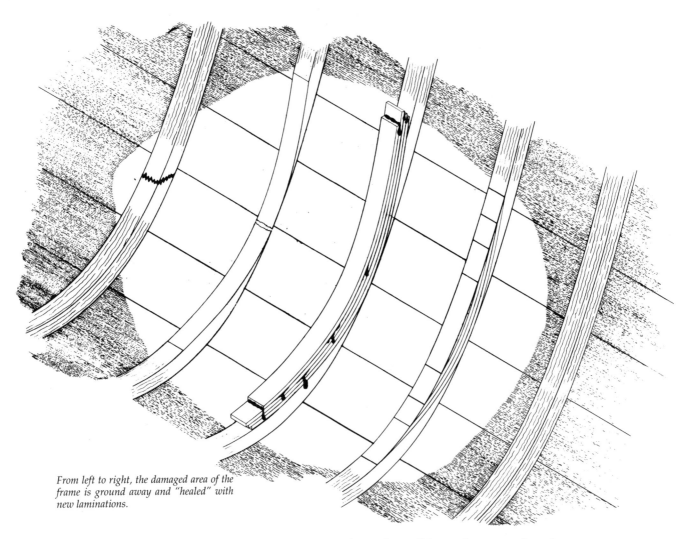

From left to right, the damaged area of the frame is ground away and "healed" with new laminations.

leaving the good parts alone and laminating in a section to replace the damaged part. The new section has long scarfs at the faying surfaces.

To repair a frame using this method, first mark a point on either side of the break that is at least eight times the molded thickness of the frame away from the break. Make up a strip of wood that will bend easily in a curve touching the planking and passing through the two points marked, as shown on the drawing. Mark this curve on both sides of the frame. Using a grinder, remove all the wood above the line, being careful not to dig into the planking. Some caution is called for here, since the grinder may cut very fast on small frames. Remember not to put the weight of the grinder on the work; instead, lightly brush it against the wood, using your grip to restrict the depth of each cut. If you have trouble controlling the grinder, an orbital disc

sander will be easier to use, but slower.

If necessary, smooth the surface with sandpaper to acceptable gluing standards, then laminate with strips to fill in the space. Finish up by smoothing with a plane and a sanding block to the siding and molding of the rest of the frame. A compass plane will be useful for shaping the curved inboard face of the frame.

The result is a good-looking repair, one that minimizes the disruption of the boat's interior, is very fast, and doesn't require much skill. Our tests indicate that these repaired frames are as strong as the originals and, when broken, break no differently than the originals. While no repair method should be taken as infallible until it has passed the test of time, we feel this small innovation is worth adopting as a standard repair technique.

New Floors and Frames

— by Samuel F. Manning —

The following drawings are a visual record of the restoration of a New York 30 racing-cruising yacht, designed N.G. Herreshoff and built by the Herreshoff Manufacturing Company. The principles apply to any other wooden boat, large or small, constructed in the same manner.

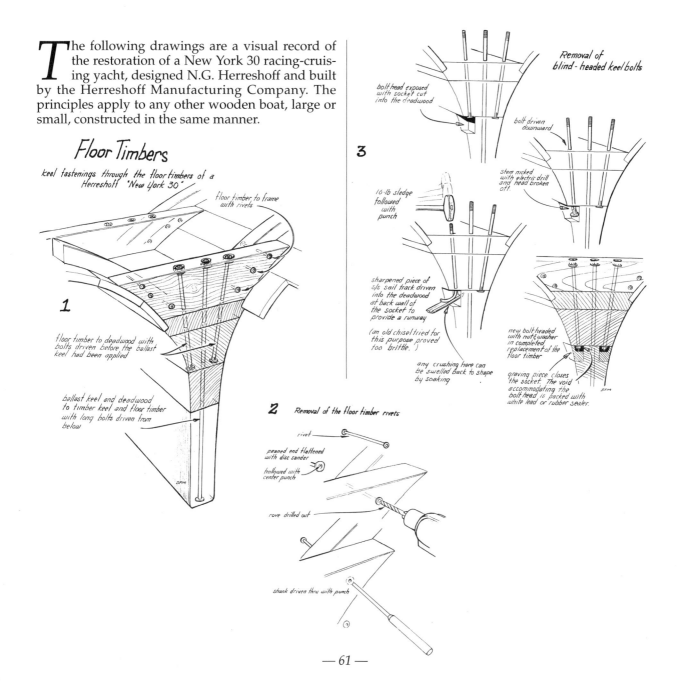

Floor Timbers

keel fastenings through the floor timbers of a Herreshoff "New York 30"

floor timber to frame with rivets

1

floor timber to deadwood with bolts driven before the ballast keel had been applied

ballast keel and deadwood to timber keel and floor timber with long bolts driven from below

2 Removal of the floor timber rivets

rivet

peaned end flattened with disc sander

hollowed with center punch

rove drilled out

shank driven thru with punch

3

bolt head exposed with socket cut into the deadwood

Removal of blind-headed keel bolts

bolt driven downward

stem nicked with electric drill and head broken off.

16-lb sledge followed with punch

sharpened piece of s/s sail track driven into the deadwood at back wall of the socket to provide a runway

(an old chisel tried for this purpose proved too brittle.)

any crushing here can be swelled back to shape by soaking

new bolt headed with nut & washer in completed replacement of the floor timber

graving piece closes the socket. The void accommodating the bolt head is packed with white lead or rubber sealer.

New Frames

The shape of new frames

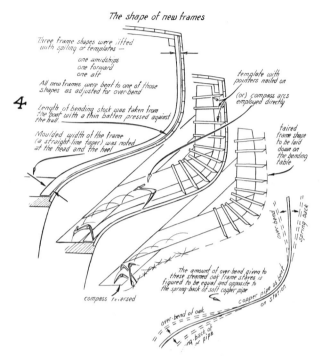

Three frame shapes were lifted with spiling or templates —

one amidships
one forward
one aft

All new frames were bent to one of those shapes as adjusted for over-bend

Length of bending stock was taken from the boat with a thin batten pressed against the hull

Moulded width of the frame (a straight-line taper) was noted at the head and the heel

template with pointers nailed on

(or) compass arcs employed directly

faired frame shape to be laid down on the bending table

The amount of over-bend given to these steamed oak frame staves is figured to be equal and opposite to the spring-back of soft copper pipe

compass reversed

over-bend
spring back

over-bend of oak
copper pipe as bent
on station
spring back of oak or pipe

4

Bending new frames

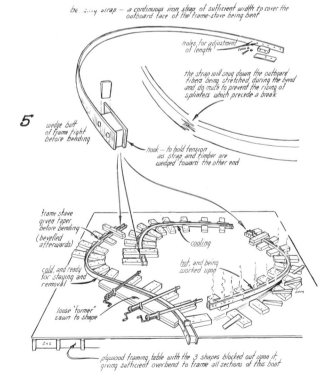

bending strap — a continuous iron strap of sufficient width to cover the outboard face of the frame-stave being bent

holes for adjustment of length

the strap will snug down the outboard fibers being stretched, during the bend and do much to prevent the rising of splinters which precede a break

wedge butt of frame tight before bending

hook — to hold tension as strap and timber are wedged towards the other end

frame stave given taper before bending (bevelled afterwards)

cooling

hot, and being worked upon

cold, and ready for staying and removal

loose "former" sawn to shape

plywood framing table with the 3 shapes blocked out upon it, giving sufficient overbend to frame all sections of this boat

2 x 6

5

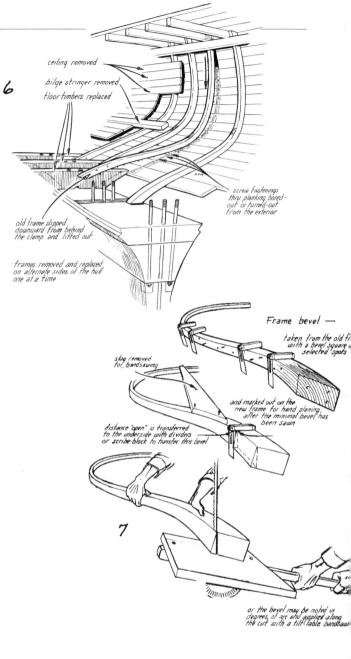

ceiling removed

bilge stringer removed

floor timbers replaced

6

screw fastenings thru planking bored-out or turned-out from the exterior

old frame slipped downward from behind the clamp and lifted out

frames removed and replaced on alternate sides of the hull one at a time

Frame bevel —

taken from the old frame with a bevel square at selected spots

and marked out on the new frame for hand planing, after the minimal bevel has been sawn

stay removed for bandsawing

distance "open" is transferred to the underside with dividers or scribe block to transfer this bevel

7

or the bevel may be noted in degrees of arc and applied along the cut with a tilt-table bandsaw

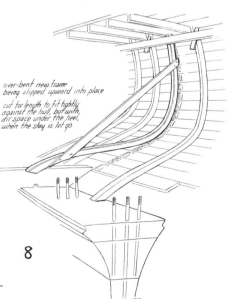

over-bent new frame being slipped upward into place

cut for length to fit tightly against the hull, but with air space under the heel, when the stay is let go

8

Gazela's New Timber

—————— by Peter Boudreau with photographs by Bill McAllen ——————

Gazela is a big ship: 320 tons displacement, 131 feet long on deck, 17 feet draft. In the fall of 1991, we at Peregrine Woodworks (a.k.a "the ship doctors of Baltimore") were hired to work along with the Philadelphia Ship Preservation Guild in accomplishing major repairs to the bow and stern of this more-than-a-century-old Portuguese-built barkentine. Besides the work itself, we were to be responsible for the drydocking that was to take place at nearby Fort McHenry Drydock #5.

The drydocking facility at Fort McHenry had not been in full operation for many years. The equipment was in very rough shape; we overhauled just

about everything, except for the gate (a huge, riveted-steel plug that keeps the water out when the ship is docked). Dealing with colored slime, rotten timber, rusty boltheads, and growing grass on the floor of the dock, we lowered to the floor by crane four 14- by 24-inch timbers, 40 feet long, to serve as the base for a system of sliding bilge blocks that we had devised.

Gazela's hull is so deep that, when she's in drydock, she looks as if she should do anything but stand up. The bilge block system functioned very well, but for peace of mind we added many poppets; we shored, we wedged, and we nailed. After a 13-hour day, the dock was pumped out and *Gazela* was secure. During the project, she would encounter 65-mph winds; she'd vibrate, but she wouldn't move.

Gazela Primeiro was built at Cacilhas, Portugal, in 1883. Legend says that her timbers were cut from a forest of dense pine planted by Prince Henry the

At the bow, the top portions of both the inner and outer stems required renewal. The old stem was left in place for a time, however, to hold the vessel's shape until the new cant frames were fitted and fastened. This photograph shows those new cant frames after they had been planed fair with the original stem rabbet. You can also see a little of the new ceiling (primed with red lead) and a 5:1 scarf being cut where the remains of the old inner stem will connect with the new 8-foot-long upper section. (The outer stem has been removed.)

Working from patterns taken off the ship and from the recorded shape of the old stem itself before it was removed, Scott "Scooter" Gifford fashioned a new outer stem, shown here as it is being lowered into place. Straps around the newly installed knightheads hold this timber close to the hull while it drops into place. Scooter's 10:1 curved scarf joint fit so well the first time that you couldn't insert a hacksaw blade anywhere along it. The new outer stem extended from the bowsprit downward nearly to the forefoot, making for a very long piece.

Navigator. Through 1900, the ship carried cargo; after that year, she was modified for fishing on the Grand Banks. Her fishing career was long and distinguished; through 1969, *Gazela* made roughly 68 round trips from Portugal to the Grand Banks.

Gazela was purchased in Lisbon by the Philadelphia Maritime Museum in 1971 and crossed the Atlantic to her new home, where she was laid up. The impetus of OpSail '76 got her sailing again for four seasons. In 1981 she was given to the Penn's Landing Corporation to serve as window dressing for the revitalized Philadelphia waterfront. The early 1980s were hard years for this fine vessel. She got worse fast.

Things began to look brighter in 1986, however, when *Gazela* was hauled at Caddell's Drydock in Bayonne, New Jersey. Her entire bottom — some 7,000 square feet in area — was recoppered with 18- by 48-inch pieces of 24-ounce sheets. By then, the Philadelphia Ship Heritage Guild was in charge of the vessel, a new name — *Gazela Philadelphia* — appeared on her stern, and a sailing program was in the works. But, according to a 1988 condition survey, she needed extensive structural work. The survey indicated that most of the rotten wood in the vessel was concentrated at the bow and the stern above the waterline, specifically from the catheads forward and from the mizzen chainplates aft on both sides of the ship. We were hired to deal with it.

We began by removing about 30 feet of topside planking, starting at the stem, and opened up an even greater area by plank removal from the mizzen chainplates aft to the transom. Ripping out

this deteriorated wood was, beyond question, some of the most depressing work that I have ever done. The hull frames, now exposed, were very rotten from the deck edge downward; some were in need of renewal to below the waterline. Aft, the rot extended inward from the framing to the beam shelf and the first three strakes of ceiling as well.

With heavy heart and furrowed brow, I took out my "master shipwright's" chalk and marked the damaged timber for removal. In the process, I had to sacrifice some perfectly good planks in order to "chase" rotten frames and yet keep the butts between planks spread out from each other. The time-honored rule is that there must be at least three frame spaces between butts in adjacent strakes of planking, and at least three strakes of planking between butts that fall on the same frame. Butts in the frame futtocks were also spread: where possible, we replaced each damaged futtock in its entirety; otherwise we established a minimum futtock overlap of 3 feet.

Access to rotted areas also required that we remove the transom planking as well as covering boards, rails, and rail stanchions adjacent to the affected areas. For "remove," read "rip out" and "discard." Wooden ships, especially those fastened with iron, cannot be taken apart piece by piece like an automobile, and then be reassembled afterward using the same timbers, no matter how carefully one works. Of necessity, removal requires destruction all the way, and our tools of choice were chainsaws, splitting wedges, mauls, and a custom-made spike puller. Working simultaneously on both ends of the ship, however, this opening-up phase was soon behind us. We were ready to fashion and install new frames, planks, and other timbers.

Here, at the after starboard side of Gazela, *two new strakes of 6-inch-thick ceiling have already been installed. Hidden behind them is a new section of 9-inch-square beam shelf, which was jacked and beaten into submission, then fastened with ¾-inch galvanized bolts. The worker in the foreground is making new frame futtocks. In sawn-frame construction, the 7-inch-thick futtocks are doubled to make 14-inch frames. While most frame spacing is about 19 inches, the areas where the chainplates fasten through the topsides are framed solid, so this is very heavy timbering, indeed. In the background, a futtock pattern of plywood is being checked for fit against the hull ceiling.*

The new 4-inch-thick planks were got out of both longleaf yellow pine or Douglas-fir. Because of available lengths of raw stock, they are a little shorter than some of the original planks, some of which were 50 feet long. Our longest plank, cut from the available 40-foot-long stock, was about 37 feet. We softened each plank, after it was made, by steaming it. Here, one of the shorter planks is about to enter the steam box from which it will emerge sufficiently pliable to be bent and/or twisted around Gazela's *frames.*

We had difficulty clamping the planks to the frames, because the vessel's ceiling was in place and therefore conventional C-clamps could not be used. Our blacksmith made a dozen massive ceiling clamps that worked very well, but they were so stressed that at the end of the project many were bent and stripped beyond further use. (They could have been bigger and stronger, but then they probably would have been too heavy to lift.) A couple of these special ceiling clamps, which were attached to the hull by lagbolts, are shown here, along with another favored tool — a length of steel pipe — as we coerce the end of a shutter plank into place.

One of the longer planks is en route to the hull from the steam box. Back aft on the vessel, planking was a nightmare, with many planks requiring up to 80 degrees of twist. It sometimes looked like those planks could not possibly be made to fit, but with our various urgings, they all complied — eventually.

The new frames were cut for a close fit to the existing ceiling, but extra wood was left on the outboard faces of the frames to allow for later fairing. The topmost futtock of each frame, known as a top timber, runs above the deck to support the bulwark, as shown here. Although the futtocks were through-bolted where they butted each other, and drifted (blind fastened) near the deck edge, we used wooden trunnels to hold them together everywhere else. Trunnels are great — especially in areas where you may have to bore later for chainplate fastenings.

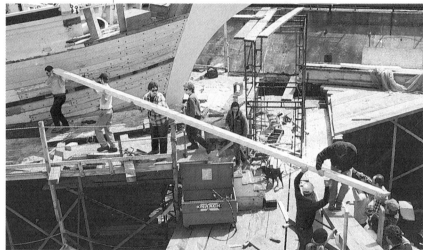

Gazela's plank fastenings above the copper line are galvanized steel spikes, shown here being bored for and driven. (Below the copper line Gazela is fastened with silicon bronze.) One man holds the spike set, a second drives it against the spike with a maul; a third man, working ahead of the other two, bores for the spikes with a combination twist drill and counterbore. Two spikes are used at each crossing of plank and frame, then the clamps are removed and bungs are driven to cover the spike heads and protect them against rusting.

The plank seams were caulked with both cotton and oakum. The cotton went in first, followed by oakum, to nearly fill the seam. Before the seams were primed with paint and puttied flush, the cotton/oakum combination was firmly set by a two-person team, one member holding a horsing iron — a caulking iron on a handle — in the seam and the other driving against it with a beetle, which is a heavy wooden maul. Here, the longitudinal seams have been caulked with cotton (except for under the hawsepipe, where the seams have been finished), and the seams at the hood ends at the stem rabbet are being widened a little so caulking can be driven there.

Work on the transom took place after the topside planking was finished, so the new hull planks could run out. Notice that there are shores under the overhanging stern; these bear against the unaffected planking and keep the vessel's after end from drooping while our work is done. As with Gazela's topsides, we found rot in the stern; here, we're in the process of replacing it.

Skill and care are required to replace a piece like this. Here, foreman John Tohanczyn fits a section of the transom rim. He is relying on a couple of temporary supports to hold it in place for fitting, and a good eye to ensure a fair curve. When all the necessary stern framing is finished, the projecting ends of the hull planking will be trimmed and mitered, and the transom itself will be replanked.

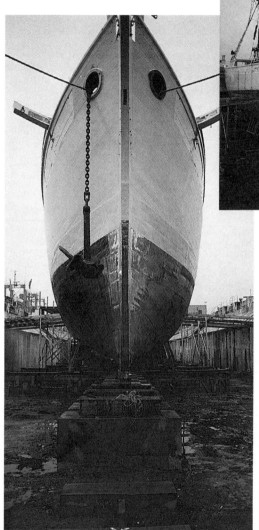

The short time frame and budget constraints resulted in enormous pressures on our shipwrights and the equipment they used. More work remains if Gazela is to sail into the next century, but as she is eased out of the graving dock on May 18, 1992 after some six months of hard work, our crew of 14 who helped breathe life into the soul of this grand old lady have reason to feel proud of what they had achieved.

A new billethead was one of Gazela's finishing touches. Here, I am fairing these carvings to the surrounding wood of the gammon knee.

The Repair and Replacement of Stems

by Willits Ansel with drawings by Kathy Bray

The stem of a wooden vessel is often the first part that requires repair or replacement. Stems are vulnerable to rot, suffer damage from collisions and groundings, and are subject to the straining and opening of seams. They take a lot of abuse, but not forever.

There are great variations in stem design and construction. They can be steam-bent in smaller boats; made of natural crooks or knees; made up of a number of sawn pieces scarfed together and fastened with drifts or bolts; or laminated from several strips of wood. In a skiff or sharpie, the stem may be a single piece with a rabbet to receive the hood ends of the planks. In a large vessel, the stem can be a complex assembly of pieces forming an outer stem, apron, knees, and gripes — the whole joined to the keel and keelson.

How Stems are Damaged

Stems are often massively built for strength, with heavy timbers closely spaced and the whole structure held together with many fastenings. This strength built into the forward end of a vessel can contribute to conditions that foster rot. Rot attacks stems at the head, where fresh water enters unprotected end-grain, and at the level of the deck, where the kingplank butts against the stem. Below the deck, ventilation is often poor; conditions are wet, dark, hot, and stagnant in the ends of vessels. Sometimes a collision bulkhead can seal off the peak, eliminating ventilation altogether. Such an environment is optimum for the growth of rot fungi.

Rot

Collision

Leaking stopwaters

Open joints

Grounding

Leaking bolts

STEM

KNEE

GRIPE

KEEL

Repairing a Stem

New stopwaters in leaking scarf joints (Stopwaters are softwood dowels driven across joints in way of the caulked plank rabbet)

A new stemhead to repair a rotted or damaged one

A graving piece, or dutchman, to repair a chafed stem

and wood deterioration can begin.

Joints in the stem can cause wood shrinkage problems, particularly if the boat is hauled frequently and dries out. When the wood shrinks, the joints open, and open joints cause leaking and general weakening of the structure. Stopwaters, of course, are placed across scarf joints to prevent leaking, but oak knees and stems do not seem to take up and swell to their original dimensions when they are repeatedly soaked and dried.

Stem joints can also be strained by the tension from a forestay or bobstay in an older boat that has been sailed hard. In extreme cases, the bolts in the scarfs will be bent and stretched, and the joints can open to the point where stopwaters are displaced and the stem leaks copiously as the boat is underway.

Surveying the Stem

One checks the stem for damage and rot in the same way one surveys the rest of the hull: probe with a knife or an awl, and tap the wood for soundness. Check the stemhead, and the inside face of the stem at the deck around deck planking seams and knightheads. Clean out and inspect the areas inside the garboards, and probe around bolts and fastenings. Look at the hood ends for sprung planks. Take out bungs or putty to inspect the heads of fastenings, and back out some of the fastenings to check them. Eye the fairness of the stem profile to find cracks in the stem; check the fairness of the rabbet line in light stems.

When a boat hits something, it's often the stem that receives the blow. The impact can cause damage to the leading edge, crack stem pieces and knees, and strain joints and fastenings.

Besides collision damage and rot, stems suffer from fastening corrosion and from the deterioration of wood around metal, particularly if the boat is iron fastened. Fastenings are concentrated in the stem; there are drifts and bolts holding the assembly together, as well as the plank fastenings themselves. They all provide a place where corrosion

If you find damage, you need to make some decisions. What repairs to make depend upon the extent of damage, the use to which the boat is put, and the amount of available time, money, materials, tools, and skills. A damaged or rotted stemhead can be recapped by scarfing a replacement piece on top. Minor damage to the leading edge of a stem can be repaired by fitting a dutchman. If the stem is leaking through the joints, sometimes driving an additional stopwater, or caulking, or tightening the bolts can stop the leak. Or, as an even more expedient measure, one can simply pack the joint with rubber seam compound. In other cases, extensive damage or rot makes replacement the only solution.

Preparations for Replacement

If replacement of the stem is called for, measure, sketch, make patterns, and perhaps photograph the old stem before removing anything. Show the stem profile on the patterns, as well as the rabbet line, the location of fastenings, and bevels. Record sided and molded dimensions where they can be measured. Do it now, before you've pulled the stem out — maybe in small pieces.

While the stem is being replaced you'll need to find a way to hold the shape of the bow to prevent it from spreading. For a light hull, a form can be made to fit around each side of the bow, or ties can be nailed or clamped across the gunwales. Often line wrapped around the bow to hold it together will suffice. Larger hulls will require shores and perhaps threaded tie-rods through the hull, with blocks, washers, and nuts at the ends. If the hull has a strong breasthook and deckbeams, there can be little spreading to cope with. But in some cases it may be necessary to force open the hood ends of the planking slightly while removing the old stem and fitting in the new one. The hood ends of carvel-planked boats can become more flexible if the planking seams are reefed out some distance back from the stem.

Pulling Out the Old Stem

Removing an old stem requires care and patience. Care must be taken to avoid damaging the hood ends of the planks, or damage to knees, aprons, and parts that are to be saved. If the plank fastenings are screws, it may be possible to back these out and remove the stem in one piece, an advantage since you can then use the old stem as a pattern for the new stem. But if the fastenings are nails, or screws that won't back out, they must either be drilled out or the stem must be taken out in pieces, the wood being chiseled and bored out around the stubborn fastenings. Usually some of the fastenings are sawn off, and some are worked back through the holes in the ends of the planks. Hacksaw blades, needle-nose pliers, and Visegrip pliers are useful tools in this long and painful process. The pieces of the old stem should be saved for samples.

The stems of larger vessels are sometimes removed by using a chainsaw to split the stem down the centerline. The gap made by the sawcut makes removing the wood on either side easier. Besides the stem itself, the apron, fore gripe, and/or stem knee — if installed — may have to come out if they are rotten or damaged. Drifts and bolts should be backed out as the wooden pieces are removed.

With tearing out completed, patterns (stiff cardboard, plywood, or thin pattern stock) can be made of the stem itself, the knees, and other parts. These should show the rabbet line, the apex, and the bearding lines. The patterns can be held up in place to check the fits at scarf joints and to check the hood ends of the planking with the marked rabbet line.

Steam-Bent Stems

Steam-bent stems are used in canoes, whaleboats, some catboats, and in some classes of lightly built smaller boats. Steaming weakens wood, and some steam-bent stems crack after years of use. If replacement is necessary, a light stem can be steamed and bent around dogs or blocks nailed on a bench or on the floor. The profile of the inside of the stem is drawn and the blocks nailed along it at intervals; blocks should be placed closely where the bend is most severe. As it dries, a bent stem will straighten somewhat unless a stay is nailed across it; some overbending may be applied. The usual considerations with respect to oak bending stock apply here: the wood should be green, clear, straight-grained white oak, with the annual rings tangent to the direction of bend.

For heavier bent stems, a more rugged form than dogs or blocks on the bench must be built. A bending strap with ends that hook around the ends of the piece to be bent will increase the chances of a successful bend. (See Chapters 2 and 17.) The strap prevents wood fibers on the outside surface of the bend from separating.

Bending stock can be boiled or steamed. The steaming rig for a light stem can be quite simple: a Coleman stove or a kitchen stove for heating water in a clean gasoline can with a spout, a hose, and a metal downspout with rags stuffed in the ends will suffice for a canoe stem. Bending a heavy stem will require more heat, such as that provided by a plumber's propane bottle, as well as a bigger boiler and a wooden steam box or a cast-iron pipe.

The rabbet can be cut in the stem before or after bending, though it's a bit easier to lay out the lines after bending. Some steamed stems have a kerf sawn up from the bottom; the kerf makes bending easier. When they're riveted after bending, these stems tend to hold their shape, whereas those without the riveted kerf will have a tendency to straighten.

Laminated, Natural-Crook, and Built-Up Stems

Preparing a laminated stem is similar to bending a steamed one. The laminations are bent around blocks secured to a bench. It's wise to put wax paper on the bench to avoid gluing the stem there permanently. Resorcinol glues seem to adhere better to oak than the epoxies do. Rabbet, scarf, and bevels are cut after gluing.

Stems that are not steamed or laminated are cut from natural crooks, or are made up of sawn pieces. In the latter instance, through-sawn planks, either from the butt of the log or farther up, may have sweep to the grain, which can be put to advantage when marking stem pieces from the patterns. A curved stem is stronger, of course, if the grain follows the curve. Seasoned wood is more stable than green wood, but if the wood is unseasoned, the application of raw linseed oil or Cuprinol followed by red lead primer on the end-grain helps reduce checking and warping. However, shrinking and opened joints usually follow no matter what when green wood is used.

If the stem is to be made of a single natural crook, place your patterns on the stock and position them to make the best use of the grain. The stem is most easily cut on a bandsaw; without one, it is a case of hewing, sawing, and planing, some of which will probably be necessary even with a bandsaw. The rabbet lines, apex, and bearding line may be laid out on pieces of the stem with the help of patterns and samples saved from the old stem. Generally, some additional work on the rabbet with a chisel is necessary as the stem is fitted.

Preparing the Planking

The hood ends of planks can sometimes be patched around fastening holes with epoxy thickened with sawdust and small dutchmen. But if the end is damaged beyond patching, the plank must be removed or cut back and replaced. Rather than drilling new holes, use the same fastening holes if the wood around them is strong enough to hold the plank; otherwise, place fastenings farther back from the ends. If the need for this is anticipated, it is worth considering making the bearing surface between the apex and the bearding line wider on the new stem than the old by making the sided dimension of the stem or apron greater. If the hood ends cannot be patched, one alternate

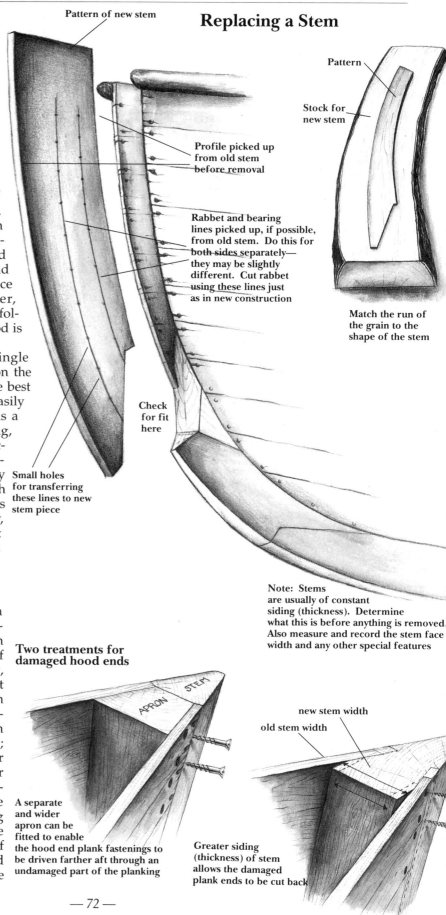

Replacing a Stem

Pattern of new stem

Profile picked up from old stem before removal

Rabbet and bearing lines picked up, if possible, from old stem. Do this for both sides separately— they may be slightly different. Cut rabbet using these lines just as in new construction

Small holes for transferring these lines to new stem piece

Check for fit here

Pattern

Stock for new stem

Match the run of the grain to the shape of the stem

Note: Stems are usually of constant siding (thickness). Determine what this is before anything is removed. Also measure and record the stem face width and any other special features

Two treatments for damaged hood ends

A separate and wider apron can be fitted to enable the hood end plank fastenings to be driven farther aft through an undamaged part of the planking

new stem width
old stem width

Greater siding (thickness) of stem allows the damaged plank ends to be cut back

solution is to cut them back and shorten the boat by an inch, or place the rabbet line of the new stem an inch or so aft.

Putting in the New Stem

The stem or knee is usually attached to the keel with bolts, or in the case of smaller boats, with rivets. These are backed out when the old stem is removed. To avoid boring more holes, the same holes through the keel are used again by drilling back through them into the new stem. If the wood of the keel around the bolt holes is split or rotted, the keel may have to be cut back or graved out with dutchmen and plugs fitted and glued so new holes can be bored where the wood is sound. And if the keel must be cut back, the stem assembly must be redesigned with a lengthened knee.

When your stem pieces are ready, put them in place and check them for fit. The hood ends of the planking usually have to be sprung open to get the stem in place; the knee and the apron may be more easily fitted if you work from inside. When you're fitting a stem in a larger boat, shores, ropes, or a come-along attached to the stemhead can help hold the stem in place while it is fastened.

You won't be able to place stopwaters to their best advantage when you've replaced the stem. Normally, stopwaters are placed across a seam at the apex of the rabbet before planking. This can't be done if the stem is being replaced, and the planks cover the point where the stopwater should be placed. One solution is to bore for the stopwater through the caulking seam; in other words, at the rabbet line where the seam crosses it. Then caulk across the stopwater.

When the stem is in place, fastened, and stopwatered, it is ready for caulking. If the seams between the planks were reefed out, these are caulked first, with the tails driven into the stem rabbet. Then a strand of cotton is driven along the caulking seam of the stem rabbet on top of the tails. Finally, the fastening holes are bunged or otherwise filled, the seams are payed and filled with compound, and the whole is ready for painting.

It is not always an easy task, but repairing or replacing the stem is often the first big task you'll have to face as your wooden boat ages. And the one that will continue its life.

A New Stem and Frames

by Maynard Bray with drawings by Kathy Bray

The decades-old knock-about sloop *Whippet* was completely restored by Benjamin River Marine in Brooklin, Maine, a few years ago. Many of the repairs that were undertaken are common to most older boats and are worth recounting here, because the techniques used can be helpful to others when working on projects of their own.

Whippet is one of nine Winter Harbor 21-class sloops, seven of which, including *Whippet*, were built by Burgess & Packard of Marblehead, Massachusetts, in 1907 for the Winter Harbor (Maine) Yacht Club. The design was by Alpheus Packard, a gifted designer who had worked for the Herreshoff Manufacturing Company and who in 1907 teamed up with Starling Burgess.

Two more boats, built in the 1920s by George F. Lawley & Son, brought the fleet total to nine. Most remarkable about this class is that, even after some mid-century apathy, all nine boats are back in Winter Harbor racing together. Several, like *Whippet*, have been restored and refurbished, putting the class on firm footing for years to come. In 1989, the Winter Harbor 21 owners were honored as the first recipients of the William Avery Baker Award at Mystic Seaport Museum's annual Yachting History Symposium.

Stem Replacement

1

The ballast keel, the entire deck, and several planks have been removed in preparation for their replacement, as well as most of the frames, the stem, the transom, and the after keel. While *Whippet* is in this weakened condition, her hull shape has to be retained by some means. Here, three external molds and a shore under the forward overhang do the job and leave the hull interior uncluttered for the task at hand. Mold shapes were taken off the lines plan. The boat's sheer, which had sagged over the years, was pushed up forward and aft about 1½ inches to

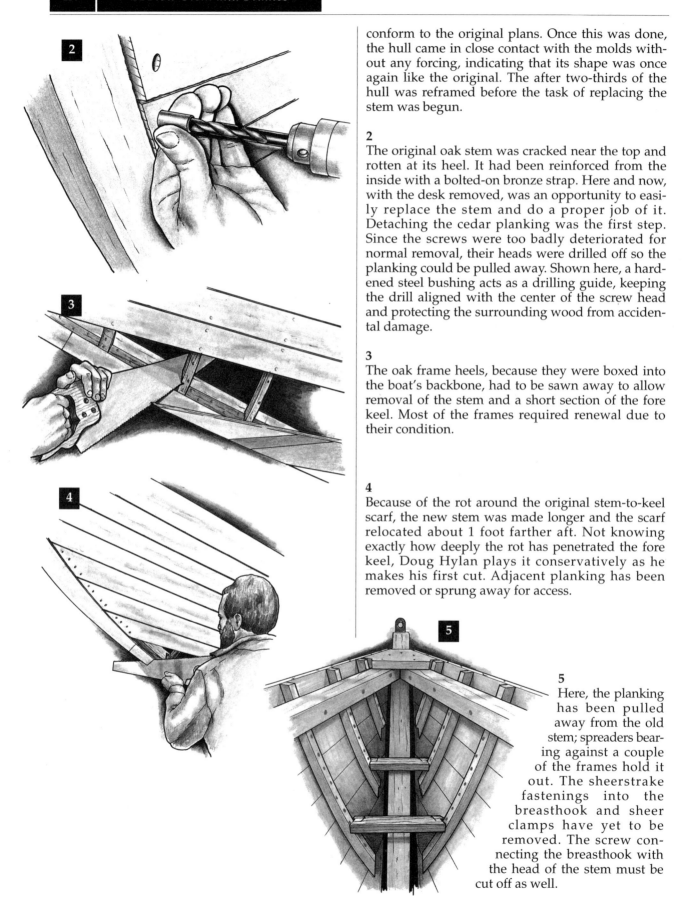

conform to the original plans. Once this was done, the hull came in close contact with the molds without any forcing, indicating that its shape was once again like the original. The after two-thirds of the hull was reframed before the task of replacing the stem was begun.

2

The original oak stem was cracked near the top and rotten at its heel. It had been reinforced from the inside with a bolted-on bronze strap. Here and now, with the desk removed, was an opportunity to easily replace the stem and do a proper job of it. Detaching the cedar planking was the first step. Since the screws were too badly deteriorated for normal removal, their heads were drilled off so the planking could be pulled away. Shown here, a hardened steel bushing acts as a drilling guide, keeping the drill aligned with the center of the screw head and protecting the surrounding wood from accidental damage.

3

The oak frame heels, because they were boxed into the boat's backbone, had to be sawn away to allow removal of the stem and a short section of the fore keel. Most of the frames required renewal due to their condition.

4

Because of the rot around the original stem-to-keel scarf, the new stem was made longer and the scarf relocated about 1 foot farther aft. Not knowing exactly how deeply the rot has penetrated the fore keel, Doug Hylan plays it conservatively as he makes his first cut. Adjacent planking has been removed or sprung away for access.

5

Here, the planking has been pulled away from the old stem; spreaders bearing against a couple of the frames hold it out. The sheerstrake fastenings into the breasthook and sheer clamps have yet to be removed. The screw connecting the breasthook with the head of the stem must be cut off as well.

6

The old stem, now free from restraining fastenings, is simply lifted out of the boat. Although a considerable portion of *Whippet*'s hull overhangs the forward-most support, which consists of a shore to the shop floor, there's really very little weight involved. The planking's inherent stiffness and its tie-in to the sheer clamps and the breasthook are adequate support at this stage.

7

The end of the fore keel will be cut back once again beyond what's shown here in order to arrive at sound wood. The new scarf will run aft from that point. (The cut-off piece was taped to the stem to make a more accurate pattern.)

8

Since Doug had made a pattern to conform to the after face of the old stem while it was still in the boat and had determined that the old stem had not changed shape during its removal, he used it as a pattern for the new one. The wood for the new stem was selected for sweeping grain — important because of the extra length of the stem — and was sawn roughly to shape to allow it to spring, as heavy timbers like this often do. Then, as shown here, it was marked precisely to the finished shape and sawn a second time. After this, planing and spokeshaving will smooth it for a finished appearance.

9

Now that the molded shape of the new stem matches that of the old, the next operation is to mark for and cut the planking rabbets and to dress down the stem outboard of the rabbet lines to the correct face width. Arbitrary station lines, squared across both the old and the new stems, provide references for transferring measurements.

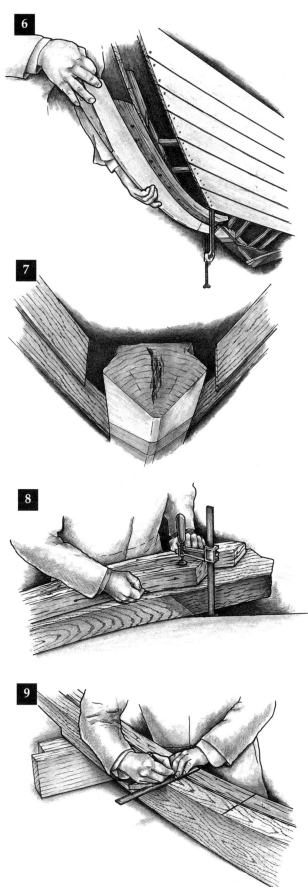

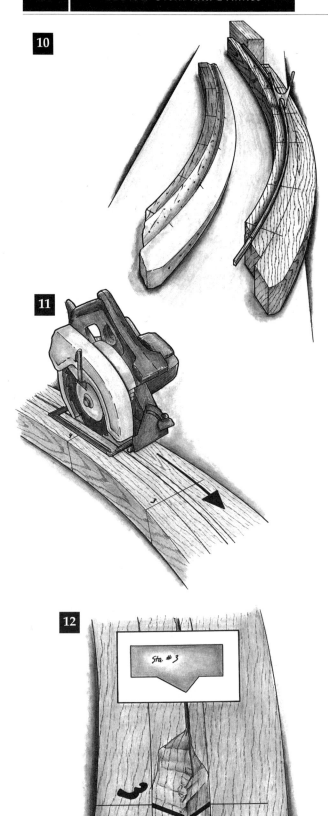

10

Measurements at each station were taken from the after face of the old stem to the rabbet and bearding lines, and these were marked on the new stem. These marks were then connected and faired, and a continuous pencil line was made with the flexible batten shown here. This same measuring and marking operation is carried out, of course, on the other side of the new stem as well.

11

From here on, *Whippet*'s stem is completed just as if it were being installed in a new boat. In cutting the rabbet, it often helps to run a continuous saw kerf, as shown; this makes roughing out the rabbet with a chisel much easier. The depth of the cut should be about one-half the plank thickness; for most boats it should be located about a quarter to a third of the distance from the rabbet line to the bearding line.

12

If you're sure you can depend on the rabbet and bearding lines, you can use a short length of planking stock as a guide for cutting the rabbet. This is the approach most builders take. But if, as here, there is any uncertainty, a cardboard template can be made (see inset) for the shape of the rabbet at each station. Once the correct shape of the rabbet at each section is determined, a marker line drawn across the rabbet serves as a guide when the rest of the rabbet is cut.

13

Now that the new stem is nearly ready for installation, it's time to cut the scarf in the fore keel, which, as you remember, must be moved aft several inches. Since there is no space for a saw to be used along the scarf, the quickest way to begin the scarf is to make a series of cuts across the timber and to the correct depth. This is done, of course, after the scarf's outline has been marked on both sides.

14

Again, because of limited access, a chisel is used to chip out wood between the saw cuts; then a plane and a spokeshave are used to work the scarf down to its lines. Using measurements and a pattern, made earlier, that represents the after face of the stem, a mating scarf is cut on heel of the new stem. Any subsequent fussing for a perfect fit was done on the stem portion of the scarf, since at this stage the stem can be tried and removed, and its scarf fine-tuned on the bench.

15

Trial fitting of the new stem is done as often as necessary to achieve a good fit at the scarf. Note that Doug has worked the stem to the correct face width outside the rabbet line; he has also soaked the stem with oil to reduce checking. The hood ends of the planking have been cleaned up so they will bear well against the new stem.

16

Here, the new stem is temporarily held in place by clamps while its fit is checked and made as perfect as possible.

17

With the stem-to-keel scarf fitted and the two parts clamped tightly together, Doug bores for a stopwater, just as in new construction.

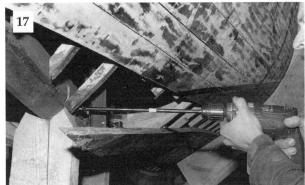

18
The holes for the bolts that will hold the scarf together are bored during this, the final fitting. Frame-heel pockets have been roughed in and will be marked at this time for their final outline...

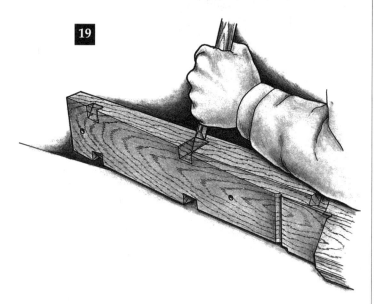

19
...and cut on the bench, where it is more convenient to work. The rabbet near the scarf has been rough-cut and will be dressed down and faired to its final shape after the new stem has been bolted into place.

20
Here is the new stem, clamped and ready for bolting, with the spreaders about to be released; this will allow the hull planking to spring in against the rabbet and become flush and fair with the rest of the hull. The scarf joint and stopwater have been bedded in polyurethane sealant, and the entire stem has been coated with red lead.

21
Because the new stem was carefully reproduced, it fits very nicely, requiring almost no reshaping of the planking to achieve a narrow seam at the rabbet. And because great care was taken in preserving the original screw holes in the planking, new ones were not required. Renewal of the frames in this part of the boat is next in line for *Whippet*; then come new sheerstrakes. An extra shore has been placed under the new stem to help maintain the desired sheerline during these operations.

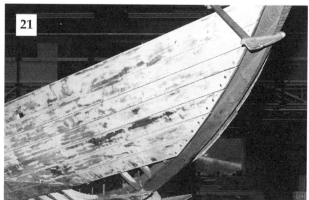

Seam-Reefing Techniques

As a prerequisite to reframing the hull, all of *Whippet*'s seams had to be cleaned of the putty and caulking that, over the years, had enlarged many of them. Reefing out seams is a chore faced by many for a variety of reasons. This method, devised for *Whippet*, may be useful in reefing the seams of other boats as well.

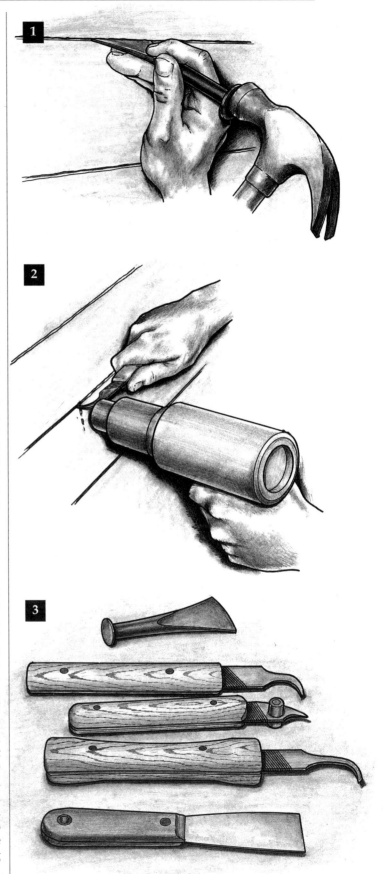

1

Instead of being tugged out with a reefing hook as is the most common first step, *Whippet*'s hardened putty is broken free of the planking from the outside by driving a caulking iron ("a") against the putty as shown here. This way the wood is less likely to be chipped away at the plank's vulnerable outer corner than if it were hooked outward. The caulking iron's face should be ground or filed until its width is equal to or a bit less than the width of the seam.

2

Softened putty is ever so much easier to remove than putty that is rock hard, and a heat gun — the type used for removing paint — is just the tool for softening it. Only a few seconds of heat is required, after which the wide and shallow putty hook ("b"in Figures 2 and 3) can be drawn along the seam to remove the putty. The putty hook, formed by the bent-over tang of a medium-size file, should be filed or ground to the full width of an average seam. Its depth should be that of the putty, because at this stage only the putty is being removed; the caulking will come later.

3

These are the seam-reefing tools. All of them, except tools "a" and "e," were made from an old file heated red hot for bending, rough-ground to shape, reheated, and plunged in oil to temper them. They were then sharpened to their final shapes on a stone. Tools "a" and "b" have already been discussed. Tool "c" is for reefing out the cotton caulking, which, now that the putty has been removed, can be hooked out fairly easily with little fear of damaging the planking. Tool "d" is a hook for scraping away traces of old putty, especially from seams that were wider than average at the outset but which were brought together during the reframing and refastening that followed. This tool should be filed to the shape of the desired finished caulking seam; a little heat might be required when using it. Sharpen the hook occasionally —putty is hard and dulls the edge. The edge of a putty knife was used to remove paint from inside as planking was being clamped together.

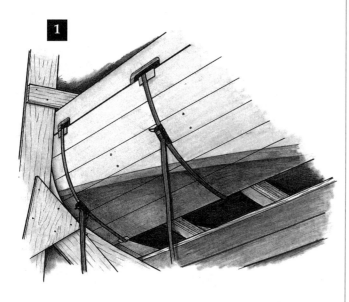

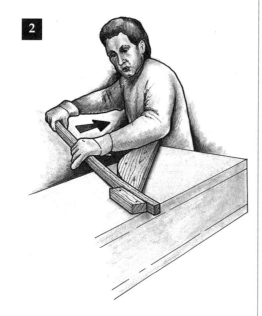

Framing and Refastening

Although *Whippet*'s frames were mostly unbroken, they had been weakened with age, and were rotten and checked in places. In spite of extensive refastening, the planking no longer lay tightly against them. A thorough reframing was called for.

1
The seams in *Whippet*'s bottom planking, especially at the turn of the bilge, had opened over the years and had become too wide to be caulked properly — a common problem in many older carvel-planked boats. Because *Whippet* was to be reframed over nearly all her length, here was a chance to pull the planking together during the process and close the seams; a new and wider plank at the bilge was then fitted to compensate. Nylon strap-type clamps, fitted with aluminum channels as bearers so as not to crush the wood, were used to pull the planking together. (The sheerstrakes, as mentioned earlier, required replacement, so they were not included in the squeeze.)

For this approach to be effective, the planking has to be pretty much adrift from the frames. *Whippet*'s strapping and squeezing took place when she was at her loosest — that is to say, when every other new frame was in place but only temporarily fastened at the center of the squeeze, and the alternate frames (the ones between them) had been removed but not yet replaced. With the hull so loosened, it was possible to begin the strapping amidships as shown and, after completing the framing and fastening there, move on toward the bow and the stern.

2
Steam-bending the frames was pretty straightforward, each one being pre-bent as shown before being offered up for installation. The crew at Benjamin River Marine made one new discovery in technique, however. In order to lie closely against the hull planking, *Whippet*'s frames had to be twisted — a difficult operation at best even in new construction. While in a new boat the frames can be splayed (i.e., allowed to lie in a natural curve) to minimize their twist and make them fay against the planking without gapping or beveling, splaying was not an option here since the original fastening holes in the planking were to be reused. Instead, the frames were pre-bent sideways before being pre-bent to the curve of the hull. Thus, it became like bending a frame that had been spiled to a shape that would fit tightly against the hull and take on the proper twist quite naturally during the process. (See sidebar.)

3

Since the sheer clamps were still in place, they had to be pried away from the sheerstrakes a little so the hot frames could be pushed between, as shown here. Each frame was slipped upward until its lower end cleared the boat's keel timber, then driven downward to seat its heel into the pocket cut into the side of the keel. (The frame heels were sealed with red-lead primer beforehand to retard the migration of moisture and rot.) Although the inside surface of the hull planking was faired as necessary for a landing surface, there was still a clear indication of the old frame's location to use to position the new one.

4

Until temporary fastenings were driven, the new and still-hot frame was held against the hull with props braced against a strongback, as shown. Although *Whippet*'s planking would be permanently fastened to the frames with copper rivets, drywall screws were driven as temporary fastenings only where necessary in the center of the squeeze area. Later they would be backed out, the holes would be properly counterbored, and a rivet installed.

Because *Whippet*'s most recent fastenings had been set so deeply into the planking, the holes had to be repaired before they could be reused. They were filled with a mixture of epoxy resin, microfibers, and microballoons to approximate the hardness of the surrounding cedar planking, then bored out again just as in new wood. It was found that priming the raw wood with plain epoxy resin before filling provided a better bond.

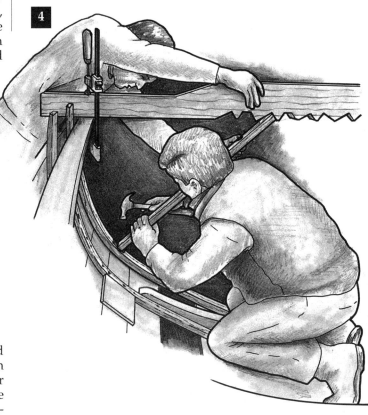

A New Twist on Bending Frames
by Doug Hylan

We started reframing *Whippet* amidships, where there is little twist to the frames and the bend at the bilge is fairly moderate. I knew that as we proceeded to the ends of the boat, especially toward the stern, the twist would make things more difficult. I figured that a few easy bends amidships would provide a good shakedown of our procedure.

We wanted to reuse the original fastening holes in the planking. These planks were over 80 years old, and I didn't want to perforate them any more than absolutely necessary. Also, we wanted the boat to look as much as possible like she did on the day she was first launched. The Winter Harbor 21s have almost no ceiling, so the frames are exposed to view. We wanted to preserve the beautiful, marching progression of curves that must be high on the list of reasons for owning a traditionally built wooden boat. So, there was no easy way out of the twist problem.

In new construction, you have lots of stout ribbands to clamp your frames to, and your movement is not restricted by the sheer clamp. So, you can usually twist and bend reluctant frames into place. On *Whippet*, we removed a plank at the turn of the bilge in the hope that a C-clamp at either side of this opening would induce the necessary twist. But as the amount of twist increased, this cure soon passed by the wayside. We proceeded quickly through an unsatisfying series of tools, techniques, and powerful words, and had begun to think about removing each frame after it cooled to bevel it, when the ultimate solution came along. It was something that Maynard Bray had recently heard about from Sonny Hodgdon, and that had long been used in the Hodgdon yard in East Boothbay, Maine.

To understand this solution, it is best to imagine yourself standing just outside your undecked boat, back aft where the twist is severe, and sighting down along a frame from its head to its heel. You will see that the frame appears to bend markedly forward in its middle as it also bends around the transverse sectional shape of the hull. In order for the frame to stay in a transverse plane as it bends around the hull and still be in contact with the planking, one corner has to bend more than the others.

As it turns out, to create this type of compound bend is simple: As the frame comes out of the steam box, pre-bend it as you normally would, then rotate it 90 degrees and pre-bend it again. (The direction you rotate the hot frame depends on whether you're working on the port or the starboard side of the boat.) After a little practice, you will find that frames so bent will lie perfectly against the planking with astonishingly little effort. The same technique should work equally well in new construction and will eliminate having to apply any twisting force to the frame.

Replacing a Powerboat Stem

—— by Jonathan Wilson with photographs by Laurie White ——

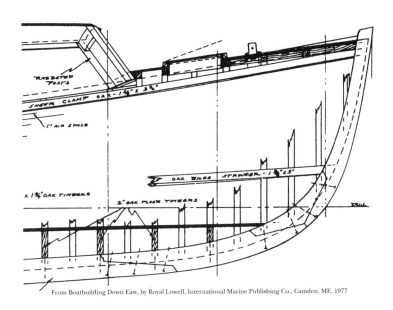

From Boatbuilding Down East, by Royal Lowell, International Marine Publishing Co., Camden, ME, 1977

The 44-foot Bunker & Ellis powerboat *Kittiwake II* had developed rot around the stemhead and along the rabbets where the hood ends of the planks were fastened. Water — mostly fresh — had gotten into the structure where the deck is fitted to the stem, and it had leaked down along the rabbets. Plank fastenings were no longer able to hold. The entire assembly was in need of immediate attention if it was not to become worse. The owner of the boat, surveyor Giffy Full, decided that replacement of the stem was the best course of action. The crew at the Brooklin Boat Yard in Brooklin, Maine, did the work. The following sequence of photographs shows how the operation progressed.

1

The first task was to sound the hood ends of the planking to determine the extent of the rotten wood. This rot was then dug out, allowing the crew at the yard to determine how many planks, and how much each of these planks, had to be cut back. With that, the paint was stripped, revealing the locations of all the plank fastenings that had to be removed in order to free the stem. The stem iron is already off in this photograph.

2

Guard irons and guardrails were also sprung out to allow for the stem's removal, as were the bolts that fasten the stem to the stem knee at the forefoot; those bolts lie on the staging plank in the right foreground. The spray rails were simply cut away forward to make the job easier. Here, Mark Littlehales is removing plank fastenings.

3

A variable-speed power screwdriver, carefully handled, makes the job of removing the screws much easier — as long as the slots in the screw heads are cleared beforehand.

4

In the absence of the power tool, a bit brace with a screwdriver bit will also make fairly quick work of the job.

5

Prying the hood ends away from the stem can be tricky if you're trying to save the planking. In this case, the crew was intent on springing an entire panel of planks a little at a time, as opposed to springing individual planks, for which it would have been easier if the seam compound and caulking had been first reefed out.

6

Working slowly down the stem after the fastenings were removed, the crew was able to open the bow enough to allow the stem to be slipped out.

7

The shape of the boat in the stem area is such that the planks tend to remain almost in the position they normally take, without additional support. If the shape were fuller, or if the job were more complicated and time consuming, this area would no doubt have been supported in such a way as to prevent undue strain on the remaining structure.

8

Here, the view is from inside the forepeak, looking forward to the ends of the sheer clamps, the plank ends, and the frames.

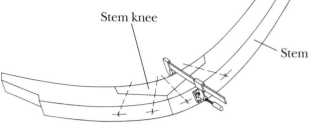

Stem knee

Stem

9
The stem was brought into the shop, where its shape could be traced on a piece of oak of suitable thickness. The unpainted portion on the inside of the stem at right is where the stem knee was bolted to the stem, as in the drawing. The knee provides for the sweep from nearly vertical to a more horizontal orientation. On the left, it is just possible to discern the discoloration of the deteriorated wood in the area of the deck — the original cause of the problem.

10
After the pattern was traced on the new oak, the blank for the stem was cut out on the bandsaw. Reference marks for the stemhead were made in order to see where the plank rabbet would stop.

11
With the original stem as a reference, the points indicating the rabbet were carefully and precisely marked, and a batten was sprung fair along these points to establish the sweep of the rabbet.

12
Three lines drawn on the new stem. From the outermost they are: the rabbet, the inner rabbet (or back rabbet), and the bearding line. The shape and location of these lines were determined by the shape of the boat at the stem, which dictates the angle at which the planks converge on the stem. Here, Peter Chase, having taken the bevel at his location from the original stem, transfers that bevel, via a bevel gauge, to a pocket in the new stem. A temporary block of wood of the same thickness as the planking proves that the rabbet has been cut deep enough when the angle of the bevel gauge is matched and the forward corner of the block is flush with the stem.

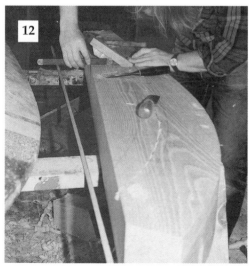

13

The process is continued at enough locations on the stem to ensure that the pockets can be connected by chiseling carefully between them.

14

Near the foot of the stem the rabbet was left a little more rough, so there would be plenty of wood left to fair into the old stem knee, still in the boat, ensuring a smooth transition. Here Peter roughs out that area of the stem.

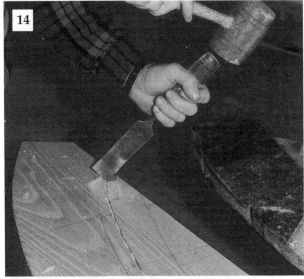

15

Once the rabbets were cut on each side, the oak was painted with red lead primer. The new stem is now ready for final fitting and shaping.

16

A block and tackle was used to help hold the stem in position as it was fitted and fastened to the stem knee and to the breasthook, above. Note that the primer on the sides of the stem has been planed off in the final shaping. Because of the way the planking fairs into the stem, the stem will be planed fine once more before a new coat of primer is applied.

17
The profile of the new stem in place.

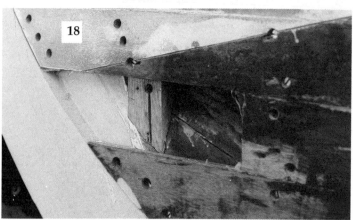

18
Here is a close-up view of the foot of the stem where it joins the stem knee, just visible at the heel of the exposed frame. A one-part polysulfide compound is used as bedding in the joint between the stem and the knee.

19
A C-clamp is used to hold a plank in place against a frame for fastening home; a plywood pad prevents the plank from being marred.

20
Here, new bronze fastenings are set up to be driven home in the old screw holes where the wood is still sound. Plugs driven into the old screw holes allowed the new screws to take hold properly.

21
The old planking on the port side is nearly all fastened back in place. New sections of planking were later scarfed or butted, where necessary, on both sides, and the structure was all buttoned up as good as new. The tarpaulin provides a shade against the destructive drying heat of the early summer sun.

Bending Stems

—————— by Edward F. McClave with drawings by Kathy Bray ——————

Rangeley boats are double-ended, round-bottom lapstrake rowing boats with a long history used on Maine lakes for sport fishing. Although early ones may have had natural-crook stems, by the late nineteenth century the straight-grained oak stem had become standard, with spruce being substituted for oak later on. The Rangeley boat stem is in two pieces, similar to that of a dory, with the beveled (inner) stem fastened to the top of a pine keel and the cutwater attached to the stem, to cover the plank ends (see Figure 1).

Most of the surviving Rangeley boats seem to have suffered at least minor problems caused by splitting of these straight-grained stems. When building eleven Rangeley reproductions at Mystic Seaport a few years ago, we wanted a stronger, longer-lasting stem whose grain more nearly followed its shape. After considering laminated, built-up, and natural knee constructions, we settled on solid steam-bent stems of white oak.

Steam-Bending is Not New

Steam-bent structural members began to come into use in American small craft around 1800, when the need for a strong but lightly built open boat developed in the whale fishery. Bent frames were introduced early on by whaleboat builders, followed by the use of bent oak stems in at least one shop as early as the 1820s. By 1850, bent timbers were commonplace in other small boats, especially in stock-built, mass-produced working and pleasure craft.

The development of compression-bending techniques in 1852 led to experimentation with bent frames

and knees for large vessels. In the latter part of the nineteenth century, the use of machine-bent timber was commercially significant.

Although not widespread, the use of big steam-bent timber was particularly common in the construction of government vessels and those powered by steam engines. The technique was most popular in the larger shipyards in the New York and southern New England areas, where the supply of natural crook timber had run out. In the late 1800s, when these yards switched enthusiastically to iron construction, and the wooden shipbuilding activity moved to less heavily capitalized yards in

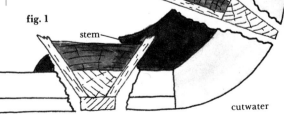

fig. 1

keel

shoe

stem

cutwater

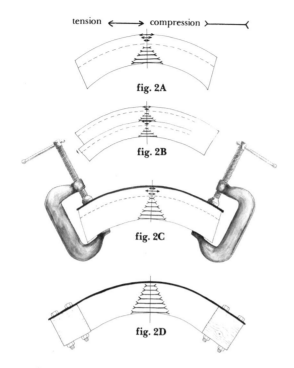

tension ←——→ compression ——→

fig. 2A

fig. 2B

fig. 2C

fig. 2D

Maine, the use of bent timber died out in large ship construction.

Bent components continued to find widespread use in the pleasure boat industry. By 1880, bent frames were the rule rather than the exception for pleasure boats and sailing yachts up to 30 feet long. In some of the larger shops, such as Rushton's, stems as well as frames were steam-bent. Herreshoff, too, used bent stems, as well as bent frames and knees almost exclusively in yachts to 50 feet long. Their light weight, high strength, flexibility, durability, and efficient use of materials and labor, especially in high-production situations, made bent components commonplace on all levels of the boatbuilding business.

The Theory of Wood Bending

When a piece of hardwood is steam-bent freely, that is with no restraint on its ends, the fibers deform as shown in Figure 2A. Those fibers on the convex side stretch while those on the concave side compress. Those about two-thirds of the way from concave to convex surface are not deformed at all. (This no-deformation zone, or neutral surface, is not in the middle as one might imagine, since steamed wood compresses more easily than it stretches.)

Under ideal conditions (straight grain, steam at 210 degrees Fahrenheit, and moisture content at 25 to 30 percent) the outside fibers of a stick of white oak can stretch about 3 percent before breaking. This deformation corresponds to a bending radius, measured to the concave face, of about 10 times the thickness of the stick; in other words, a 1½-inch piece can be bent to about a 15-inch radius before breaking.

Several bending methods are available that make tighter bends possible. The simplest is the saw kerf (see Figure 2B), which, if centered, allows a bend to half the original limiting radius. The kerf, of course, needn't be centered, nor should it be in some cases. For example, in a screw-fastened frame the kerf is best located slightly toward the convex side to allow the screws to get a good bite into the inner part of the frame. In a rabbeted stem, the kerf should be sawed to fall completely inside the apex, or inner rabbet line, eliminating the possibility of leakage along the kerf. The minimum possible bending radius is about 10 times the thickness of the largest segment after kerfing. Keep in mind that saw kerfs need only run through the sharpest part of the bend, so the thickness of the piece at any given point relates to its desired radius as 1 is to 10.

A metal strap clamped to the outside (convex) surface of a timber before bending reduces split-off surface fibers and allows a slightly tighter bend (see Figure 2C). However, pieces bent this way, especially if the tightness of the bend is pushed past the normal free-bend limit, have a tendency to break in service. The strap, while limiting stretch in the very outermost fibers on the convex face, does not restrain those fibers beneath the surface. The resulting shear stresses that are set up between fiber layers can eventually stretch the outside fibers past their breaking point.

The most effective method of attaining a tight bend is by bending with end restraint, or by what is commonly called compression bending. In this process the piece to be bent is fitted tightly between blocks attached to a strong metal strap, and the entire assembly is bent as one, the strap being on the convex side of the bend (see Figure 2D). The strap, which does not stretch significantly, prevents virtually all stretch in the wood fibers, so the convex side fibers are not deformed at all, while the concave face of a piece may compress 25 percent or even more without failure. This process allows bends with a radius to the inside of the curve as small as three times the thickness of the piece.

We used compression bending for the Rangeley boat stems, which were 1¾ inches thick and with a radius of 6 inches at the tightest part of the bend. We had no serious failures in any of the 22 bends.

The Wood for Bending

For the Rangeley boat stems we used fast-grown white oak cut from the butt logs of trees a foot or more in diameter whose rings were generally ¼ inch to ½ inch apart. Such trees are found where the ground is moist all throughout the growing season. This wood not only seems to bend more successfully than slowly grown oak, but also it is denser when dry, and therefore stronger and more durable, having a higher ratio of dense, late growth (summer wood) to porous, spring wood.

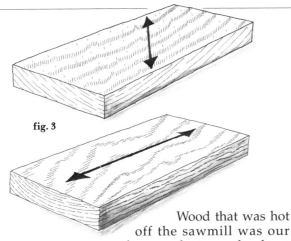

fig. 3

fig. 4

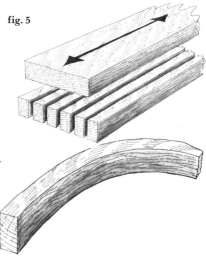

fig. 5

Wood that was hot off the sawmill was our preference, but we also bent some oak that had been aged for a few months. There was no noticeable difference between the two in the ease of bending or in the success of the bend. However, bending oak must be stored very carefully if it is to retain its qualities. Such wood should be stored in the board (not pre-cut into bending blanks), sticked, and covered to protect it from too-rapid drying, which can cause surface checking, with the ends well painted to prevent end checking. Seemingly minor surface checks, which may form in a matter of hours on green wood that is not properly protected, can cause bending failures.

Bending oak can also be kept absolutely green by sealing it up in plastic bags with salt water and kerosene. We stored sawn-out frame stock, ⁵⁄₁₆ inch by ⅝ inch half-round, this way for months with no drying occurring whatsoever. But be sure to use salt water. One time, when we were too lazy to walk to the river for it and substituted tap water instead, we ended up with a batch of frames covered by a lush crop of mold after a time in the bags.

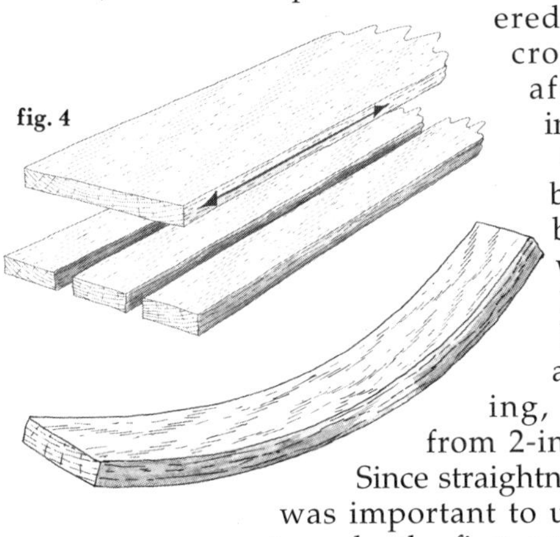

Our stem-bending blanks, which were 1¾ inches by 3 inches after planing, were cut from 2-inch boards. Since straightness of grain was important to us, we took care to make the first cut as close to the grain direction as possible, even if it was quite far from being parallel to the edge of the board.

Finding the true grain direction isn't always easy. The intersections of the rings or rays with the surface of a board do not always indicate the run of the wood fibers. The direction of the pores is the grain direction, and should be the primary indicator (see Figure 3). In our case, since we were bending as in Figure 4, and since we had no control over the most important grain direction — that on the edge of the board — if a board had bad grain on its edge, we didn't use it for bending.

Sometimes better bending stock can be gotten out of the edge, rather than the flat of a board, provided the board is thick enough, because as shown in Figure 5, one has more control over the run of the grain on the critical surface.

The alignment of the annual rings in bent timbers is a popular subject with boatbuilding writers. The accepted method is to bend with the rings "on the flat" (see Figure 6A), a method that is structurally desirable if the piece in question is to be alternately wet and dry, as in the frames or stem of a boat. The swelling and shrinking in the direction of the principal fastenings (stem bolts in the case of a stem, or plank fastenings in the case of a frame) is less if the annual rings are on the flat instead of on edge. Thus compression of wood under fastening heads, upon swelling, and the subsequent loosening of fastenings when the wood dries out and shrinks, is minimized (see Figure 6B). The argument that a piece bent with rings on the flat is less likely to split along its fastenings doesn't seem to hold up, since a piece of oak is just as likely to split along a ray as along an annual ring.

Very often the required dimensions of the bending blank and the thickness of the boards of bending stock available don't allow the builder any choice in the matter of ring alignment (see Figure 4), as it was with us. We bent stems with the annual rings on the flat, on edge, and on the diagonal, and found no real differences in ease of bending or in the success rate among these three different ring orientations.

Side compression

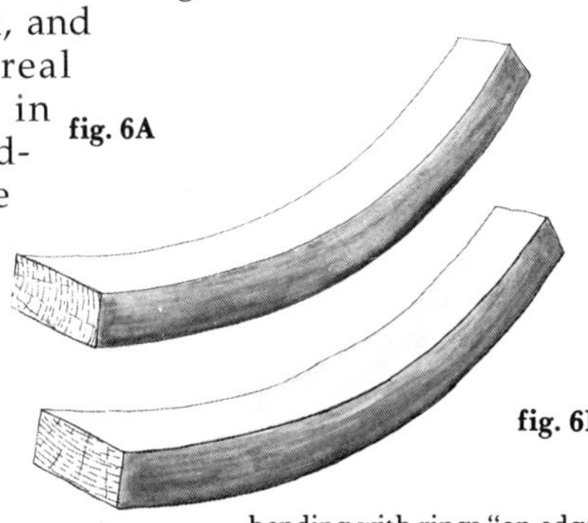

fig. 6A

fig. 6B

bending with rings "on edge"

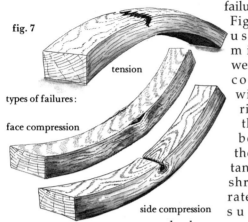

fig. 7

types of failures :

tension

face compression

side compression

failures (see Figure 7), usually minor, were more common with the rings on the flat, because the high tangential shrinkage rate made surface checks more probable on the inside of a flat grain piece than on the same surface of an edge grain stick, and these side compression failures always began at a check on the concave surface. We were lucky that the shape of our finished stem allowed us to trim these damaged places when we finally cut it to size after bending. Its sided thickness at the tightest part of the bend, where failures always occurred, was about 1½ inches, or roughly half what we started with. We found that planing the planks to thickness immediately before bending eliminated small surface checks, thus lessening the chances of failure.

The Equipment for Bending

Our steam box used freshwater steam at atmospheric pressure, and we cooked the stems for 2 to 2½ hours before bending. We had to be careful to keep standing water in the bottom of the box, or the atmosphere inside became too dry, and the stems began to check while being steamed. We also found that we had to baffle the steam hose where it entered the box, to prevent the steam jet from impinging directly on the surface of stems; this also caused checking. The ends of the stems were painted to avoid excessive softening of the end-grain, which must bear tremendous pressures during the bending process. The painted ends also provided a convenient surface for identifying marks.

We chose to use the reversed-lever method of compression bending (see Figure 8) for several reasons:

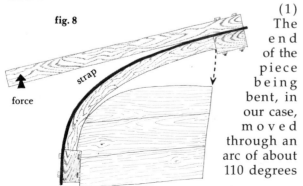

fig. 8

strap

force

during the course of the bend, and thus it would have been very difficult to consistently maintain a good lead angle for a block and tackle had we chosen that method (see Figure 9).

(2) The reversed-lever rig is quite self-contained, in that the forces exerted on the building or structure to which the form is attached are small; no strong attachment point is needed for the dead end of a block and tackle.

(3) The reversed-lever method is less likely to over-compress the piece than is the block and tackle method. (This is a complex subject that is covered in depth in the technical literature.)

One disadvantage of the reversed-lever rig is that the lever inter feres with clamping. Unless the entire bend is a uniform arc of a circle, the piece and the strap must be clamped to the form as the bend progresses. We got around this difficulty with the wedging arrangement shown in the photographs.

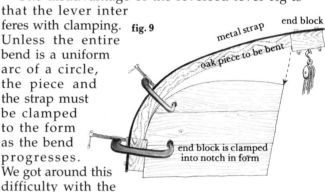

fig. 9

metal strap

end block

oak piece to be bent

end block is clamped into notch in form

The reversed lever, strap, and form are shown in Figure 8. The bending form was made up of heavy planks cleated together with plywood and was as thick as the rough stem was wide. The strap was made from a length of a large bandsaw blade, ¹⁄₁₆ inch thick and as wide as the form was thick. We ripped the teeth off this blade and dressed it to width using an abrasive wheel in a table saw, a spectacular operation that was much more exciting than the actual bending of a stem. The end blocks were of seasoned oak, securely bolted to the ends of the strap, with the grain of the blocks running parallel to the strap, and were large enough to completely overlap and bear against the end-grain of the stem blank. The lever was a 2 by 4, bolted through the free end block and reinforced near the end block with a piece of angle iron. The distance between the end blocks was slightly greater than 4 feet, and the stem blank was cut an inch or so shorter than that distance, a wedge arrangement taking up slack and straightening out the strap when in place. Without a means of wedging, it is very difficult to get the blank jammed between the blocks tightly enough to prevent some tension from occurring on the convex surface of the piece during the bend.

In addition to transverse pins and wedges to hold the stem against the form, we had several mortises chopped in the form for C-clamps. A clamp was always used to hold the free end of the stem after bending where the lever prevented wedging.

(1) The end of the piece being bent, in our case, moved through an arc of about 110 degrees

The Process of Bending

The photographs show the progression of the bend once the stick was in the strap. Our bending operation took about one minute from the opening of the steam box until the stem was bent, wedged, and clamped in place. The action was quite furious in that minute, I might add, with a lot of yelling, steam-fogged eyeglasses, misplaced tools, and swinging tools all adding to the excitement. Once we had our methods figured out, two workers could bend a stem easily, although we usually had three or four helping. If the block-and-tackle method is used, one person can bend an average small-boat stem alone.

Once the stem was bent, we began spraying it with water to prevent the surface from checking; the water also sped up the cooling process, allowing us to remove the stem from the form in about 45 minutes. When the stem had cooled to room temperature, we fastened two stay laths to the side that faced upward. The form was configured to allow these laths — we used 1- by 3-inch pine — to be fastened to the stem without our having to remove the stem from the strap or release the wedges holding it to the form. Once the top laths were in place, the stem was released and the bottom stay laths were immediately fastened on.

If a bent piece is released from the strap and form before it has cooled, even with the stay laths in place, it may twist, or tension may develop along the outside surface, making later failure possible. A stick bent to a circular arc need only have one set of stay laths connecting the very ends. If the curve is irregular, as the Rangeley stem was, several pairs of laths are needed, since, unless constrained, the stem will gradually relax toward a circular curve while drying.

Measurements taken of our stems showed that, if properly cooled before removal from the form, and if well supported by stay laths, the curves remained the same indefinitely, with no stretching along the convex surface.

No overbending was necessary. The curve of the form was exactly that of the inside of the stem. If a stem was released from the stay laths within a couple of weeks of bending, it did tend to straighten out a bit, but after being sided and beveled it was easily clamped back to the proper shape when set up on the building jig.

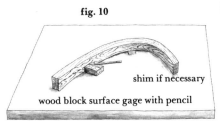
fig. 10

shim if necessary

wood block surface gage with pencil

Shaping the Bent Stem

Once the stay laths were removed, the stem blank was laid on edge on a table saw bed, and centerlines were established on the faces with a surface gauge using the saw table as a reference plane (see Figure 10). This procedure eliminated the inaccuracy that would have occurred had the lines been marked directly in from the edge of a slightly twisted stem. From these centerlines, we marked the apex line, a constant width, down the convex face, and the width of the bearding line on the concave face. The width of the bearding line was 2½ inches at the sheer, 1¼ inches at the knuckle of the forefoot, and 3 inches where the stem lapped onto the keel. We then beveled to these lines (see Figure 11), and fit a stem so shaped to each end of the keel, where they were fastened permanently. The stems were temporarily fastened to the building jig as well.

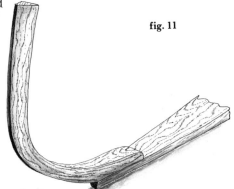
fig. 11

Some Conclusions

The use of bent stems was not only structurally desirable in the case of our Rangeley boat project, but also was economically attractive, especially when compared to the use of natural knees, which seemed to be the most reasonable alternative to bending. Eleven boats were built, each having two stems that were similar enough to enable us to bend them over the same form. The nonproductive time invested in the bending equipment was not much of a consideration to us, considering the number of pieces being produced. For another builder, however, the use of compression-bent stems might prove more expensive than other methods, even though the materials cost of a bent stem is low.

A "standard" bending might make the use of bent stems more feasible to builders in nonproduction-line situations. Such a setup would include:

(1) A bending strap, preferably of spring steel, stainless steel, or spring brass. The latter two would be better for work that is to be varnished, because the steel strap stains the wood. The strap should be about 1/16 inch or so thick, and as wide as the widest piece that might be required; it is often convenient to bend one wide piece and resaw it into two or more stems after bending. The length should allow 4 feet between the end blocks; this is sufficient length for most small craft stems and allows efficient use of 8-foot lengths of bending stock, which are more easily obtained than any other. If a very short piece, such as a seat knee, must be bent, the rig can be easily adapted as shown in Figure 12.

(2) End blocks, bolted to the ends of the strap. These can be 6 inches or so long, as wide as the

strap, and a bit thicker than the maximum molded dimension that you expect to encounter. The bolts should be set in flush with the inside face of the blocks (the face away from the strap), so the block at the fixed end can be clamped into a notch in the bending form, eliminating the need to lag or bolt the strap to the form (see Figure 9).

(3) Wedges to tighten the piece to be bent firmly between the end blocks on each end of the strap. These wedges must exactly match the molded dimension of the piece being bent. For applying the force for bending, a reversed lever can be bolted to the strap, or an eyebolt in the free-end block can be attached to a block and tackle.

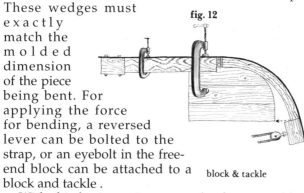

fig. 12

block & tackle

With this basic equipment and a form roughly built of scrap lumber, the techniques of compression bending can be within the means of any boatbuilder, amateur or professional.

Keelbolts: Removing the Old, Installing the New

by James Woodward

The removal and replacement of the bolts holding the ballast keel to the deadwood of a sailing craft can be one of the most difficult jobs that a restorer faces. After reading this, at least you'll know what you're up against and why.

The keelbolts, of course, secure the ballast keel, which is easier said than done. In even a 25-foot boat, the keel can weigh a ton or more; in a 50-footer, as much as 20,000 pounds might be carried. All this weight must be held firmly at all times to the deadwood, even when the boat is on her beam ends, with no shifting or movement. The bolts must sit tightly in their holes, or they will leak. If they break, anything from a costly mess to a tragic sinking will result.

Small wonder, then, that the state of the keelbolts is a topic of much discussion.

If the surveyor thinks the keelbolts are bad, the procedure for their replacement depends on the materials involved.

There are three types of ballast: lead, iron, and other. Leaving aside the exotics, such as uranium (very dense, but expensive and radioactive), "other" is likely to be concrete, with or without ferrous scrap added. Telling the three apart is not difficult. The easiest test is to hit the ballast hard with a fairly heavy hammer, which will bounce off iron with a ring. Lead will absorb the blow, becoming slightly dented; concrete will probably chip. Lead can be cut with a knife, iron cannot, and what you can do or not do to concrete should be obvious. But don't be fooled by the various surfacing compounds that might have been used on lead or iron and which superficially resemble concrete.

Surveying the Keel

If you're buying a boat; if you bought your boat without a survey; if more than five years have passed since your boat has been surveyed; if your keelbolts leak; or if you have any other suspicion of trouble, call for help at once. A good surveyor will examine the ballast-deadwood joint carefully and will bang each bolt with a hammer, listening for the dead sound of a corroded bolt. The good surveyors are remarkably accurate with such crude methods, and their opinion should not be taken lightly.

The Keelbolts

You also must determine if the bolts were cast into the keel (lead or concrete only) or inserted into holes through the ballast with a nut on the bottom. The easiest way to do this is to look for plugs, usually wood, which cover the nuts. These may be either in the bottom of the keel or in the side. If there are no nuts under all that bottom paint, the bolts are cast in. (It is also possible to drill and tap lead for bolts, inserting from the top, but these bolts may be treated as cast in place, since removing them is probably impossible.) Cast-in bolts cannot be removed for replacement, short of melting down the keel and starting over. Such a keel must, therefore, have more bolts added. Through bolts, on the other hand, may be replaced by removing the originals.

If the bolts are cast in place, nothing short of X-rays, an expensive option, can tell you more than you already know. If the bolts run right through the ballast keel, one should now be removed for inspection. This is fair to both parties in a buy-sell survey, since the removal will not only verify the condition of the bolts, but also give an indication of the degree of difficulty of removing the remainder, if such will be required.

If the bolts are cast in place in lead, drilling holes for new bolts is quite easy. Pick your locations in the deadwood where they will not interfere with fastenings already in place, and drill new holes, using an ordinary twist drill or a barefoot ship's auger, fed slowly. If simply duplicating the existing location pattern is not easy, try to put one bolt in each frame space over the ballast, using Nevins's rule (see sidebar) for sizes. If the existing bolts go through the floors, you can drill more holes in the floors, but only if there is plenty of wood left; putting them through the deadwood only will suffice, in any case.

If the bolts are cast in concrete, you have a problem. It might be possible to drill new holes, using a twist drill through the wood, and a masonry bit into the concrete. This will not be easy. If the concrete is loaded with ferrous scrap, the masonry bit will have trouble with the metal and the twist drill will get indigestion from the concrete, and you will have learned one more reason why you should stay away from concrete ballast. You might try casting a new keel of iron or lead; such a keel will necessarily be of higher density and therefore smaller to achieve the same weight as it is in concrete, so fill out the difference with wood.

With a through-bolted keel, the job is simple — just remove the old bolts one at a time, replacing each one before removing the next. As with so many things marine, this is easier said than done. The bolt was tight in the hole when it was put in; you're taking it out because it is corroded; access is difficult. Now is the time to liberally flood the exposed upper ends of the bolts with penetrating solvent. Everyone has a favorite brand; quantity is more important than the label on the can.

To hold the solvent while it works, use an empty soup can. Remove the end, place the can over the nut, and seal the bottom rim of the can to the top of the keel with bedding compound or modeling clay. Fill the can with penetrating oil, and come back tomorrow. Heat sometimes helps, but be careful not to start a fire.

Removing the Keelbolts

The traditional method for driving out a keelbolt is to remove the top nut and knock the bolt down from above, using a sledge. This is the easiest and fastest method, if it works.

There are three matters of importance. First, the corrosion of the bolt will probably be near the top. In severe cases, enough of the bolt may be gone that pounding on the top will simply compress the remainder, pushing it outward into the wood. To avoid this problem, have a helper watch the bottom while you bang away at the top; if the top can be driven down, even slightly, without a corresponding motion below, you are compressing the bolt. Stop pounding!

Second, you must drive the entire length of the bolt down through deadwood and ballast. Use only hardened steel tools or rods as drivers in the hole. Soft-steel drivers, such as bolts and drifts, will bend under the pounding and stick in the hole. A cheap source of hardened steel rod is junk automobile axles. Look for a rod with a diameter that is 1/16 inch less than that of the keelbolt, 1/4 inch less at the most.

Third, getting a good swing on the sledge may be difficult in the confined quarters of the boat's cabin. In this case, try using a metal fence-post driver. They are available from farm and garden stores, or you can make one yourself. To make your own, select a piece of steel pipe with an inside diameter slightly greater than that of your driver and of a length to suit your space. Put a pipe cap on one end and pour the pipe half full of molten lead. A propane torch will melt small pieces from a spare ballast pig, or you can buy lead wool from a plumbing supply store and pack it in without heat. To use the post driver, simply slide it down hard over your pusher and let the lead do the work; your exercise will be in lifting it for the next hit.

In any case, the goal is to prevent the top of the keelbolt from being expanded by the pounding. It's best to file it slightly before starting and keep

> ## CAUTION
> The forces involved in the removal of obstinate keelbolts can be great. Always take precautions against unexpected breakage of equipment or shifting of the boat itself. For personal protection, wear a full plastic face shield, a hard hat, and steel-toed shoes.
>
> Remember, when using a sledge, that chips can fly. When using a jack, the jack itself, the driver, or the press frame can bend; the ground it is sitting on can become compressed; the boat, rather than the bolt, can move up or sideways; and the jack can slip.
>
> Safety must be your foremost concern.

an eye on it as long as you can.

If driving downward doesn't work, try working from the bottom up. Remove the bottom nut, and use the largest jack you have to push your driver up. The same cautions about drivers and the end of the bolt apply. In addition, you must be careful to position the jack and the driver directly in line with the bolt; any misalignment here and the driver can spit out sideways with considerable speed. Wear a face shield.

Have a helper watch the boat while you work the jack. The evidence that this technique is not working will be the elevation of the boat, not the bolt. Obviously, if the boat itself is jacked up more than a little, the cradle or poppets will no longer be supporting the hull; eventually, if you keep on jacking, the boat will go over on its side.

If you see that the boat is being elevated just a little, stop working the jack but maintain tension on it, then try to break the friction of the bolt in the keel by banging on the top of the bolt, the side of the keel, and anywhere else that is convenient and effective. It is sometimes possible to help from above by loosening the nut and levering under it with a pry bar, or wrapping a chain around the loosened nut and carrying it up to a second jack or a come-along. This will certainly help, but remember that chain is never as strong as it looks. Even a small jack will be stronger than the chain; a breaking chain can injure you severely.

If you are tempted to brace the boat to something overhead to keep it from moving up as you jack from below, be sure to use a strong brace and think carefully about what you are doing. Most ceiling and roof structures are calculated to resist a snow and wind load up to about fifty pounds per square foot, distributed over the entire roof. You will be applying considerable force in one place and in the wrong direction. On the other hand, you might be able to position a Travelift or a similar device to serve as the overhead.

NOTE ON SIZES

Keelbolts are much discussed, but only one of the standard yacht design references discusses sizes. *Skene's Elements of Yacht Design* devotes considerable space to Nevins's rules for construction. Nevins specifies one square inch of keelbolt area for each 1,500 pounds of ballast, given a 60,000-psi tensile-strength bolt. This provides a 40:1 safety factor, which is certainly conservative, but not overly so. Furthermore, it seems to be in line with modern practice.

As an example, a 6,000-pound keel would require 4 square inches of bolt; using approximate figures, this could be provided by:

1 bolt	2¼" diameter
4 bolts	1⅛"
5 bolts	1"
7 bolts	⅞"
9 bolts	¾"
13 bolts	⅝"
20 bolts	½"

The best choice would be somewhere between five and nine bolts. Fewer than five will not adequately spread the load, while more than nine increases the nuisance factor. A good rule of thumb is one bolt per frame space, at a minimum, staggered from side to side, and two per frame space at a maximum. Five ½-inch bolts should be the minimum for any size keel. Avoid bolts longer than 30 times their diameter; they will be difficult to drive and to remove.

Dealing With the Toughest Bolts

If you still can't drive those bolts out, and if you have a lead keel, you will have to drill new holes (see above).

If you have an iron keel, you must choose between drilling new holes and removing the entire keel. The former is no fun, but with a good drill, several sharp bits (keep them sharp!), and plenty of oil, it will work. The difficulty of the latter varies with the size of the keel. Here, too, thought is needed, can you handle a great, unwieldy, mass of iron? Are the keelbolts vertical? If so, read on.

Block the boat so that the ballast is unsupported, with three or four inches clear underneath. If the keel is squat and rectangular, no further preparation is needed as it will rest easily when removed. But if the ballast is of a shape that suggests it could fall over when removed, a mini cradle must be built so it can be moved sideways once it is down. Remove all of the upper keelbolt nuts, any deadwood below the ballast, and any straps holding the ballast. With help from a crowbar and by banging on the bolts, the keel should move down, slowed by friction. You can now either cut the bolts with a hacksaw and move the keel sideways, or lift the boat off the ballast with a sling-type lift.

With the ballast removed, you can now work on the keelbolts, using the methods described above. You may also be able to borrow a hydraulic press (most garages have them) and press the bolts out. Don't be surprised if you start to bend even a 20-ton model. Be careful!

If all this fails, at least the keel will be accessible, allowing you to use a drill press for boring new holes. However, before resorting to that, you may be able to combine drilling out the bolt with banging down on it. The success of this will depend on the composition of the keelbolt. Since cast iron is usually softer than the steel used in the bolt, the drill will have a tendency to wander away from a straight hole. Crooked holes leak!

Replacing the Keel

When you are ready to put the keel back in place, smear bedding compound on the top of the keel, drill bolt holes through the deadwood if needed (probably from the bottom to avoid crooked holes), align the keel, and jack it up.

As for filling those hard-won empty holes with new bolts, you have a choice to make. Most authorities agree that Monel is best for keelbolts, no matter the type of ballast; it is expensive, however.

Stainless steel is a possibility in an iron keel, but some people don't like it. If you use stainless, choose Type 316 and save the paperwork to allay the suspicions of a future purchaser of the boat that you may have used a cheaper grade.

For a lead keel, silicon bronze is almost as good as Monel, and about half the price. Reject all other bronzes, including "manganese bronze" and "naval bronze" — both of these terms cover a multitude of sins. The small added price for silicon bronze will give you a much more satisfactory bolt.

In an iron keel, you can also use plain steel. This will not last anywhere nearly as long as the specialty metals, but it is much cheaper. On balance, galvanizing the steel is probably not a good idea. The only galvanizing worth buying is hot dipping, and that will reduce the strength of the threads. Do, however, apply cold galvanizing compound to the threads after installation. It comes in a spray can, contains about 95 percent zinc, and will meet various military specs for galvanizing.

Your best source for keelbolts is your propeller and shaft supplier, for two reasons: First, used shafting, if carefully selected and of the proper metal, can often be used for keelbolts. To select a piece of shaft, use a caliper to ensure there is no appreciable wear at either end of the proposed bolt, where the threads will go, or along the first six inches down from the top, where most of the future corrosion will occur. Second, a keelbolt is a great deal like a shaft. It is long, must be threaded at both ends, and is made from a type of metal that many machine shops will not be accustomed to working.

While you're giving the order, remember to get hex nuts and flat washers in the same metal for both ends of each bolt. Try to get "heavy hex nuts" rather than the more common "finished hex nuts." They cost twice as much, but will provide extra strength.

Installation of the bolts is not difficult. At both ends, you should use a canvas washer under the metal flat washer; the nut goes over both. Do not use lockwashers, as they will distort the flat washer slightly and could cause a leak. Lubricate the length of the bolt with your favorite bedding compound, put the canvas and flat washers at the top end of the bolt, and screw on a temporary plain steel nut to protect the threads. The top end of the bolt should not protrude from the nut. Now drive the bolt all the way down. Remove the plain steel nut and replace it with the permanent hex nut, lay on bedding compound, and the canvas and flat washers on the bottom, and screw on the bottom hex nut. Tighten the nut as hard as you can.

If one of the bolts is to replace an original one that lies over a crosspiece on the cradle and you can't shift the boat, you're probably safe to simply leave the old one, especially if there are eight or ten new bolts. Make a careful note in your log indicating which one you left, however, in order that some future surveyor doesn't extract that bolt and draw a faulty conclusion about the condition of the remainder.

Finishing the Job

When you finish installing all the new bolts, tighten each nut again, then again in a month, whether the boat is in use or on dry land. It is possible to overtighten a bolt and break it, or cause leaks, but the average amateur won't be able to apply that much torque. If you're using very heavy wrenches or a ¾ inch or 1 inch air impact wrench, be careful not to go too far with it.

Now make tight wooden plugs for the bottom holes, smear them with a good bedding compound, and drive them. A little extra attention here will help to avoid leaks through the bolt holes later on.

Finally, make a note in your log of the date, the number, size, and material of the bolts replaced. Save the invoice from your supplier, making sure it designates a specific material (Monel R rather than just Monel; Type 316 Stainless, not just stainless; Everdur 655, rather than simply silicon bronze, etc.). Save a tag end of the stock, if there is any left. All of this will help convince some future skeptical surveyor that you did the job properly.

Take next week off to recuperate, then go sailing.

Removing Rusted Keelbolts

by Michael Dziubinski

Rusted keelbolts in hardwood are some of the most ornery and stubborn pieces of iron ever pounded into a boat. Try to get them out, and the more you pound, the higher you bounce. The boat shakes, you shake, and the bolts stay put. What can one do in such a situation? Quit work early? Quit work altogether? Convince the owner that a ballast keel really isn't important?

Finding myself choosing among these very questions after a day of pounding and bouncing, I quit work. Early. I then happened upon a system based on the hydraulic jack — and logic.

The tools of the system are these: a hydraulic jack, some heavy bolts (¾ inch or larger), four pieces of ¼-inch by 1½-inch steel strapping, lots of old bolts and bits of rod to use as chasers, and some miscella-

neous blocks of wood for a base and bracing. The logic behind the system is this: The bolts can't be pounded down out of the boat, so why not push them up and out, letting the corroded tip lead the way, rather than the fat, scaly part at the base?

To push the bolts out this way, you'll need to find a way to resist the upward pressure of the jack, either by using the boat's own mass, or by using a force pushing in the opposite direction of the jack. This force can be an external one, such as a post between the top of the keel and a stout overhead beam. Or it can be an internal force, somehow pulling the boat against itself to resist the upward push of the jack. The latter is what I'll detail here; it was the solution chosen for our situation, because the boat proved to be too light to resist the force of the jack — it just lifted as we pushed on the bolts — and because there was nothing external to push against.

The garboards must be removed for access to the top of the keel in order to set up the "extractor." This done, the metal straps of the extractor can be hung from bolts laid atop protective wood blocks on top of the keel. We had tried piercing the keel with bolts, but found that technique put too much pressure on the keel, threatening to crack it; also, the bolts bent from the pressure, crushing the wood underneath them (that's why it is necessary to protect the keel with some wood blocking).

It is important that the base of the jack be stout and able to resist all the force you're going to need to move the bolts, otherwise the base will bend or break. The jack must also be braced down low, so the base

The Extractor

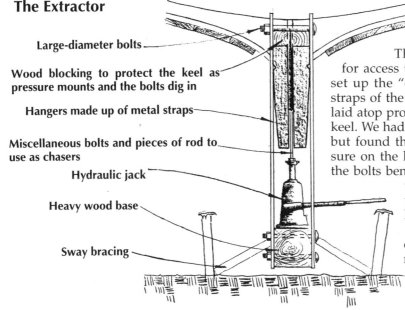

Large-diameter bolts

Wood blocking to protect the keel as pressure mounts and the bolts dig in

Hangers made up of metal straps

Miscellaneous bolts and pieces of rod to use as chasers

Hydraulic jack

Heavy wood base

Sway bracing

can't "flop" from side to side. As pressure mounts on an unbraced base, the jack wants to kick out from under the keel rather than move the bolts. If your boat is heavy enough or if you have that overhead beam, this isn't a problem, because the jack can be set on the floor or the ground, stable as can be.

After you set the rig up, it is just a matter of pumping out the keelbolts, using a flat-head bolt or a piece of rod as a chaser, or driver. When the jack is fully extended, let it down, block it up or insert a longer chaser, and start over again. A rust-loosening agent can be used on the bolts, applied from the top. We squirted it into small holes drilled into the wood around the perimeter of each bolt. (These holes were of a diameter slightly larger than that of the little red tube supplied with most spray penetrating oils.)

As it turns out, we learned a lot that day: about stubbornness, about hydraulics, about logic, and about brains over brawn. It took two men about four hours to completely pump out four very stubborn bolts that hadn't even budged in many hours of pounding the day before. Of course, the system we set up was particular to our boat and to the resources we could scrounge in the yard, so it may never be used again in this exact form. But it will always remain an idea lodged in that infinite part of us where ideas go, another seed for future problem-solving.

XX

A New Keel for an Old Boat

by Maynard Bray
———— with photographs by Anne Bray ————

*B*oat repair is very different from new construction. If you get into it, you'll soon find that it's not the series of well-established steps that are contained in books and magazines for starting a boat from scratch. Questions keep popping up: How much do I rip out and where do I stop? How do I join the new work to the old? How should the hull be held or supported while the boat is being repaired?

If you're blessed with innate good judgment for such things physical, you'll simply start the job and proceed with ingenuity, dexterity, and dispatch. But if you're among the masses with a yet-to-be-developed sense of what to do, some exposure to how others, more competent and more experienced, do such work would doubtless be welcome. There is much to be learned from the ways of others, provided, of course, that those ways are the surest and quickest path to a good job.

Here, then, is the story of a new keel for an old boat, with the cast of characters consisting of *Tarne*, a 40-foot Swedish-built ketch of 1930 with a rotten keel; Joel White, owner of the Brooklin Boat Yard, Brooklin, Maine, and its guiding light; Belford Gray, the project leader of the work on *Tarne*; Tim Horten, a good-humored young man at home with both adze and air-driven rust scaler; and Sonny Williams, a man with exceptional leanings toward helpfulness and productivity.

1

Tarne is in the shop, already torn apart and awaiting the installation of her new keel. She is supported by her bilges and on her centerline forward and aft of her keel. The defective wooden keel has been removed, along with the lead ballast keel, which rests on a cradle under the starboard bilge, and some lower planking. Six 6-inch by 6-inch posts under each bilge support the boat's weight and are braced against the walls of the shop to prevent spreading. Some keelbolts remain to be removed, since the old keel was sawn into chunks and split out, the fastest means of removal.

2

After the new keel timber has been sawn and planed to thickness (sided), a big, portable saw is used to cut wide around the marked outline. White oak was used — a fairly green piece that won't swell as a seasoned one might and cause problems when it sees service underwater.

3

Tarne's floor timbers are mostly of Swedish iron, and they and her wooden hull framing originally ran down into the side of her keel where they were pocketed and fastened. For the repair, all these projecting ends will be cut off flush and additional bolting elsewhere will make up for the lost strength.

4

While there is good access, all the metal is scaled free of rust; before *Tarne* goes back overboard it will be repainted with coal tar epoxy.

5

Establishing the appropriate bolt-hole locations on a thin plywood pattern is the next operation. These holes, cut with a hole saw, are somewhat oversize for a quick and easy fit down over the projecting ballast keelbolts.

6

Small squares of plywood having proper tight-fitting holes in them are then slipped over the projecting bolts and nailed into place on the pattern, thus establishing exactly where bolt holes must be bored in the new keel timber.

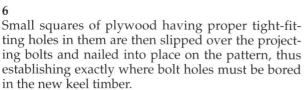

7

Once rough-cut to size and free of any stresses that might tend to pull it out of alignment, the keel is checked along its marked centerline for straightness, and a second and more precise cut is made along the marked outline. It is always a good idea to make such cuts in two steps like this.

8

Since the after end of the keel butts against the sternpost, it must be cut before the keel goes into place for its trial fit. The keel's forward end, however, can be left long and trimmed to its final shape after fitting.

9

Pieces of the old keel help in establishing what the new one should look like. This piece, for example, shows where the rabbet ends. Others show the nature of the rabbet itself as it runs aft.

10

A batten is used to mark the rabbet for cutting — the right-hand side of this batten is on the bearding line.

11

With a portable saw set a little less than the depth of the rabbet (which is roughly equal to the planking thickness), a cut is made along what will be the middle line of the rabbet.

12

Another cut is made at the correct (least) bevel along the marked bearding line, and the strip can be pulled out, revealing the rough-cut rabbet.

13

Since there is a changing angle where the planks meet the keel along its length, there will be a corresponding wind to the rabbet. These finishing cuts are made carefully with a chisel and a mallet, using as guides the angle lifted from the boat at intervals and a short piece of "plank thickness" stock as shown.

14

Tarne, being of European build, quite naturally has metric-size fastenings. Without a bit of the proper size, the yard crew could have been held up, but with some ingenuity and a torch, a slightly undersize bit was reshaped by bending its flutes outward to bore a larger hole.

15
With the hole pattern made earlier, circles are marked on the new keel where bolt holes are to be bored.

16
The center of each bolt circle is found with a pencil compass, marked, and then punched with a nail lightly driven to make a good starting place for the spur of the wood bit.

17
The ballast keelbolts have been established as being square with the top of the keel, therefore a hole that aligns with these big bolts is necessary. A couple of "sighters" using tri-squares helps keep the hole square as it is bored.

18
The new keel, with its ballast-keelbolt holes bored, its rabbet cut, and its after end trimmed properly, is slid under the boat for a trial fit and for marking of the floor timber bolt holes. The lead ballast keel lies to the right and will not be involved in this operation.

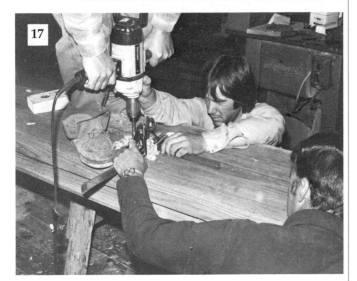

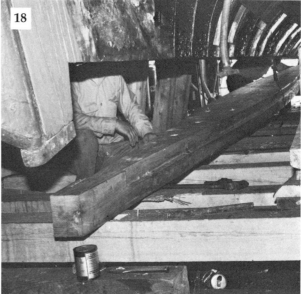

19
Up she goes — with a bit of persuasion.

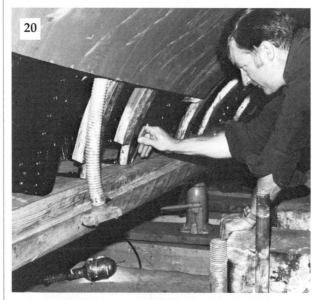

20
A bit of marking here...

21
...and saw-cutting there...

22
...a marking of the rabbet line forward...

23
...and checking for fairness where the planks land...

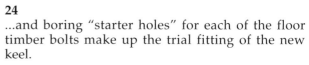

24
...and boring "starter holes" for each of the floor timber bolts make up the trial fitting of the new keel.

25
With the keel removed to a place where it can be worked on, the "starter holes" are continued through the keel timber, taking care once again that they are square with the surface.

26
Rather than the usual limber holes through her floors, *Tarne* has two limber grooves running fore and aft along the top face of her keel. Sonny Williams cuts these grooves in the new keel with a router guided by a straightedge temporarily nailed in place.

27

With the new keel turned bottom up, each of the recently bored floor timber bolt holes is temporarily plugged and counterbored so the bolt heads will not stand proud. Each bolt is then driven in with a turn or two of white-lead-soaked caulking cotton wrapped around the body of the bolt, just under the head; the cotton will prevent leaking around the bolt.

28

Here's the keel, turned right-side up again, all ready for final installation. The big holes, of course, are for the ballast keelbolts.

29

This sandwich, which includes white lead and tar paper, once fastened together, will be slid under the boat and jacked up into place for the final time. But before that is done, let's go over the work required to get the ballast keel and deadwood to the stage shown in this photograph.

30

The ballast keel had a couple of voids; somewhere in the distant past someone had seen fit to cut big chunks out of this lead casting. Perhaps it was so the boat would trim better fore and aft, but in any event, it made sense to melt down enough of her inside ballast to fill up these voids. This would make the boat more stable and the top of the ballast keel an unbroken plane surface. Temporary wooden sides were clamped in place on either side in way of the voids, and lead pigs were set into the cavity thus formed. Molten lead was then poured in to bring the level up flush with the surrounding surface. To hold these two new chunks of outside ballast lead permanently in place, short lengths of bronze round bar were driven into fore-and-aft holes in the "mother" casting — much as reinforcing rod is used in concrete work.

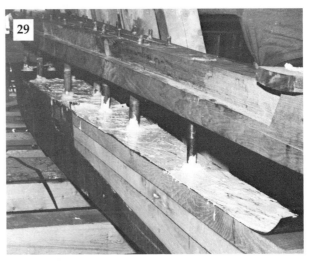

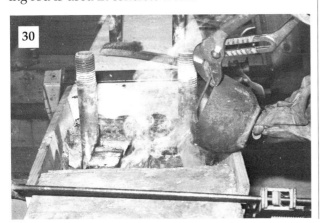

31

The deadwood aft of the ballast keel needed renewing. This was a less-than-straightforward task, because of the presence of ballast keelbolts over which the layers of deadwood must be fitted. The deadwood fills out the ballast keel assembly, so it will form a plane surface and will mate with the bottom of *Tarne*'s new keel timber and the top of the ballast keel. The new deadwood is made up of oak in three layers. For the first layer, a slab of live-edge stock with holes bored in it for the keelbolts (located by means of the plywood bolt pattern used earlier for the new keel itself) is let down into place so its outline can be marked.

32

With the first piece of deadwood marked and cut to the proper outline as traced from the ballast keel, it is wedged into position for tapering; that is, its top surface is brought parallel with the top of the ballast keel forward of it. The deadwood's forward end offset is taken...

33

...and the after end is brought up to match that measurement using a straightedge extension of the ballast keel as a reference. The lower surface of this piece of deadwood will then be scribed and cut to match the slope of the ballast keel.

34

With the top surface of this lowermost piece of wedge-shaped deadwood parallel to the underside of the new wood keel — and, of course, to the forward part of the ballast keel as well — the remaining layers of deadwood can be of constant thickness.

35
Here they are, all three layers of the deadwood clamped together for a trial fit. At their final assembly, a good, thick coat of red lead primer will be smeared on the faying (joining) surfaces as a bedding agent to fill any small voids that might exist.

36
A pattern shaped to fit where the deadwood must eventually go gives assurance of a good fit.

37
Here's the pattern tacked in place for marking on the deadwood. Often it is more prudent to prove the fit with a pattern such as this than it is to cut according to lifted measurements. Wrestling this heavy keel assembly into position under the boat is a major task, so this deadwood is not a good candidate for the cut-and-try method of fitting.

38

38

The completed keel assembly, at the far side of the hull, is now ready to be put in place. A trial fitting has already been made of the keel timber before it joined the ballast, so rolling the complete (and very heavy) assembly into place and jacking it up into position can be a one-time-only operation. The many bolts that will hold it securely to *Tarne's* floor timbers can be seen sticking up from the top surface of the new keel. They're short, because *Tarne* has iron floor timbers, and the bolts only have to penetrate their lower flanges. The iron floor timbers have been scaled free of rust and painted with a coal-tar epoxy coating to help lengthen their life. You will notice there is a piece of deadwood yet to be fitted at the forward end of the ballast keel. Don't be misled by what appears to be blocking on top of the keel assembly; what you are really seeing are some of the 6-inch by 6-inch shores beyond the keel that support *Tarne's* starboard bilge.

39

39

At the assembly's after end, where the floor timbers don't directly contact the new keel but are separated from it by existing deadwood, longer keelbolts are needed. They are being marked for here, laid out so as to miss the bolts that hold the keel assembly together and which are already in place.

40

The only access for boring these bolt holes is from up on *Tarne*'s deck. A length of common round bar is used here to extend the shank of the wood bit to reach the electric drill that powers it. The round bar is simply welded onto the bit's shank; it is held in alignment for welding with a short piece of angle iron clamped in the jaws of a vise.

41

It's a long way down to that hole in the deadwood, but if the drill is held at the correct angle (an extension of one of the lines marked in photo 39)...

42

...and the lead screw of the bit is started in the right place (as is being done here with the aid of a stick), the chances are good that the hole will end up where you want it. A barefoot ship's auger, without a lead screw, might have had less tendency to wander, and for that reason barefoot augers are the boring tools usually selected for a long but accurate passage of this nature once a short starting hole has been bored. At this point you can see that the keel assembly is in place, blocked up and wedged from underneath to make firm contact with *Tarne*'s hull. White lead paste was used as bedding between the old wood and the new.

43

With all pieces in their final position and securely bolted together, the fairing operation begins — first with an adze on the sides of the new keel assembly.

44

This is what the new keel's forward end looks like. As with the after end, there were some long bolts required here. Just why *Tarne*'s ballast keel was built the way it was, particularly at its forward end, is a bit of a mystery. It would seem better if the main casting had extended all the way forward and all the way to the bottom in one piece; this would provide some strength during accidental grounding. Perhaps it was originally built that way and was changed for some reason over the years. In any case, the keel will be put back the way it was when *Tarne* arrived in Brooklin — with a chunk of oak forming the forward corner.

45

That chunk of oak is in place here in this photograph, but has not yet been faired into the area around it. The adze marks indicate that final fairing has yet to be done on the sides of the new keel timber; that will come after the hull is planked.

46

Another chunk of oak extends the keel profile aft to the heel of the rudder. Both it and the forward fairing piece are somewhat sacrificial in that they are independently fastened; that is, the main keelbolts will not pass through them.

47

Softwood stopwaters are vital to keep water from leaking along the joints of the keel and the deadwood, and into the boat. Caulking, when driven into the garboard's rabbet, will lie across face of the stopwater if it is correctly located, as this one is.

48

Now for the planking — from the top downward to the garboard. A thin spiling batten is tacked to the frames so it takes the same lay as the finished plank will, although it need not fit tightly around its edges. In fact, the gap between the spiling batten's edge and the desired location for the edge of the finished plank is useful — it is measured at successive points and recorded on the face of the batten. These gap measurements are what will determine the shape of the new plank.

49

The spiling batten is laid out and tacked to the planking stock. Measuring back out from the specified points a distance equal to the recorded gap measurement yields the outline of the finished plank's edge. There will probably be some bevel needed on the upper edge of the plank as well, so it will fit snugly against its neighbor. In addition there will be a caulking seam running in about two-thirds the thickness of the plank and open on the outside about ⅛ inch. But we'll worry about those refinements after we cut out the basic shape of the plank.

50

Stiff lining battens are used to connect and fair the tick marks picked off the spiling batten. These lining battens, the outside edges of which represent the desired shape of the new plank, act as guides for the sawing and shaping operations. A rough cut is first made slightly outside the battens on the table saw, then...

51

...the roughed-out plank, with the battens still in place, is passed by a shaper, which, because its guide bushing bears against the edge of the batten, cuts the new plank exactly to the desired shape. In new construction, this finished plank would then become the pattern for its mate on the other side of the boat; with *Tarne* it was thought best to take individual spilings for each of the planks involved.

52

Since this part of the hull is concave, the backs of the new planks must be "rounded" to fit well against the frames. The amount of rounding is determined here by a templating tool, then the plank is worked down with a plane until it matches the templated shape in the way of each frame. Edge bevel — the angle between the lower edge of the existing plank and the frame, and adjusted to form a caulking seam — can now be determined and the mating edge of the new plank planed to match it.

53

Butt blocks come next. They're of oak, hollowed for a good fit against the planking and fastened to the existing plank before the new one is hung.

54

And now for a trial fit. (The astute reader will note that this is a different plank than the one with which we started.) The material is hard mahogany, and it takes a good bit of force to get the plank to lie where it should; that is, hard against the frames and the edge of the plank above it. The clamps and shores bring it in against the frames.

55

A close fit to its neighboring plank is achieved by a series of shores wedged against the keel rabbet. If there is any trimming needed — and many times there is — the high spots are marked, and the plank is removed and shaved down as needed. Then it is clamped back in place again before any fastenings are driven.

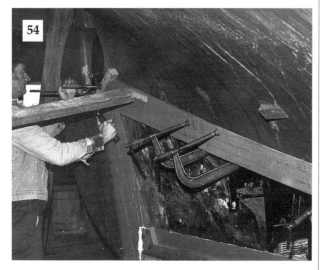

56

The plank fastenings for *Tarne* are a combination of wrought-iron bolts for the metal frames, and bronze wood screws for the oak frames and butt blocks. A ring of cotton is wrapped around the head of each bolt to form a watertight seal. The wood screws fit tighter in their holes than a bolt and, of course, aren't driven all the way through the frame, so they don't need such treatment.

57

The wrought-iron bolts used in the iron floors were made up right at the boatyard, since they couldn't be bought commercially. One bolt at a time was sawn to length from a wrought iron rod after the bolt head had been forged by heating, then peening to shape in a forming die. A threading die was then used to cut the threads on the opposite end. Store-bought galvanized nuts and washers were used.

58

As with the new keel, the new planking is roughed down to a fair surface with an adze.

59

A disc sander takes over from the adze to finish smoothing up *Tarne*'s new underbody. In skilled hands and with coarse paper, a disc sander is one of the more effective tools for such work, as it is much faster than a hand plane.

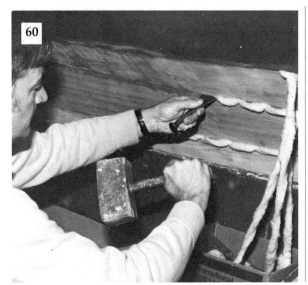

60

60

As the final step in the *Tarne* repair, the new planking is caulked. The freshly driven cotton will then be primed with paint, and the seams will be puttied out almost flush to the planking. After her bottom is painted with a couple of coats of anti-fouling paint, she'll be ready for the water.

Renewing *Tarne*'s keel wasn't cheap, or fast, or without its headaches. Somewhere around $15,000 (early 1980s), 800 man hours, and considerable planning went into the task, and although every 50-year-old wooden boat with a rotten keel wouldn't have been worth the effort, *Tarne* most assuredly was. Here was a craft whose topsides were so smooth you couldn't detect the seams in the planking, a craft that — except for her keel — had just passed a rigid survey with flying colors, and one that had had a succession of good owners. Duplicating the workmanship or the woods used to build her would be nearly impossible today.

A Keel Lamination in Place

—— by Clifton Andrews ——

Arline *rests on 2-inch by 4-inch oak supports, which free her keel for the replacement of a 12-foot section. The front wheels of the bus-frame trailer were removed to allow the bow of the 50-footer to pitch down when the rear of the trailer was jacked up.*

Most boat owners would not consider themselves lucky to have the cross member of a cradle crack and sag under the weight of their 50-foot boat and "squat out" a soft place in the keel, but we did. The accident resulted in the replacement of a rotted 12-foot section of the 5-inch oak keel that we might not have detected otherwise; it also resulted in new garboards, and the replacement of other suspicious planks in the canoe stern of our 76-year-old double-ended motorboat *Arline.*

We had hauled the boat for the winter on a new 20-foot 6-wheel trailer made from a bus frame; we were not sure exactly how far forward we should position the boat on the trailer. As it turned out, we had her too far aft. The weight concentrated mostly on the after part of the trailer was exerting so much pressure on that part of the keel that the soft portion of the keel began to be crushed, causing it to bulge slightly and make ominous sounds.

At this point, *Arline* was nearly completely out of the water on the concrete ramp. Our good shipmate, Cap'n Ken, who had made the trailer, noticed that an oak timber at the rear of the steel frame of the trailer had also cracked under the 12-ton load of the boat. Rather than risk causing more strain in the wrong places by hauling the boat farther up the ramp, Ken reversed gears and let the whole thing back into the water for repositioning. This time we

Holes for the keelbolts were drilled in each lamination of new oak, using a master pattern. The new lamination was then jacked into place.

Shingles were driven into any wide cracks in the seams between the new laminations. Later, after the new keel section was sanded, the seams were caulked with cotton and compound. A 2-inch oak worm shoe completed the job; it was recessed to cover the ends of the nuts and bolts.

nailing them to prevent slipping. To provide just a bit more room between the trailer and the hull, Ken let the air out of the tires!

Then came the removal of the punky section of the keel. This was accomplished with a circular saw, speed borers, and chisels. Fortunately, the deadwood near the planking was sound, so we could add sections down from there without having to cut away up inside.

Toward the end of the keel there were six pairs of ½-inch by 24-inch bronze bolts holding the keel assembly together. These bolts ran for about 4 feet. We installed ten more pairs along the remaining 8 feet of the keel that needed replacing.

Unfortunately, part of the section that required replacement ran under the engine, and the only practical way to put the nuts and washers on the upper ends of the new threaded rods we used for bolts was to remove the garboard strakes. It was either that or lift the engine off its bed. We wanted no part of the latter!

Removing the garboards, however, turned out for the best. We discovered all sorts of surprises when Ken applied the catspaw to the fastenings and removed 8-foot to 10-foot sections of plank. We discovered the garboard had been fastened with old iron nails, certainly there since 1900 when *Arline* was first built; they were considerably slimmer, now. We also found Monel nails and steel screws. Quite a variety!

Laminating the New Section

The former owner had assured us that the hull was built of 1-inch hard pine, and apparently most of it really was, which accounts for *Arline*'s long life. Having no local source of Southern hard pine, but with a nearby mill sawing plenty of prime, native white pine, we settled for several beautiful 1 by 10s for planking stock.

The plan was to laminate in place the new section of keel. The first layer of new oak was cut, fitted into place, and held up by small jacks. Holes were drilled up from underneath, through the section of keel remaining, for a total of 20 more ½-inch

slid the boat a good 4 feet farther forward before rehauling.

It was late in the season, so we decided to wait until spring for the repairs to the keel. In the course of his fall woodcutting, Ken spotted a white oak on his property that he figured would do just fine for keel timbers. The tree was felled, and Ken hauled it in sections to a local sawmill with instructions to quartersaw timbers that we could season over the winter.

Removing the Bad Section

When the weather moderated in March, the trailer was jacked up about 6 inches, giving us just enough room to work under the keel. We tacked ¾-inch pine planks to the hull below the turn of the bilge to distribute weight, placed others on the ground below to provide a level footing, and then installed 4-inch by 4-inch uprights of oak every 18 inches along one-third the length of the hull, toe-bolts, which were to hold the new section together and secure it to the boat.

Using a heavy-duty electric drill to bore holes into white oak while lying on your back is no breeze. In some places, because of the confined space, Ken had to dig small pits in the ground to accommodate the drill and use wooden levers to gain enough pressure to push it into the wood.

As new laminations of 4-inch oak were added, holes for the bolts were drilled in these with a master pattern, and then the pieces were jacked into place. This also proved to be tedious work, as it is not easy to bore all the holes in precisely the right places and at precisely the right angle along a 4- or 5-foot piece of wood and then force the section in place over several long bolts. Obviously, we could have avoided this complication if we had been able to raise the boat another 2 feet or so, or if we could have dug a deep trench under the keel.

Finally, the bottom lamination was socked home, the jacks were put in action to hold the entire assembly in compression, and the nuts were installed and tightened on the projecting 32 bolts. The tough part of the job was over! The exposed nuts were then capped with a 2-inch oak shoe, which was screw-fastened to the bottom of the whole assembly.

So, what should have been a simple haulout turned into the signal for major work. Undoubtedly, if the punky section hadn't been crushed, we wouldn't have noticed any problems beyond some leaking during the next couple of seasons. But there's something very satisfying in restoring this ancient vessel to robust health. As far as we are concerned, it was a lucky break.

Replacing a Keel and a Centerboard Trunk

by Maynard Bray with photographs by Benjamin Mendlowitz

Maribee, one of the well-known Buzzards Bay 15s, carries Herreshoff hull number 731. The class name comes from the waterline length of the boat — the overall length is 24 feet 6 inches — and from the body of water for which the first batch of boats was intended. Built in 1914, *Maribee* is owned by Steve Ballentine, in whose Cataumet, Massachusetts, boatyard the following repairs were carried out. What follows is the story of making and installing a new keel and centerboard trunk.

Although no rot had softened *Maribee*'s keel timber, that vital piece of oak had developed splits all along its 22-foot length — full-thickness splits that leaked, including a large one right down the middle — and were virtually impossible to make tight. A new keel timber seemed the most logical approach, and since a good piece of longleaf yellow pine of sufficient length was

available, that substitution was made with the knowledge that there would be less checking and splitting in such a timber than with oak.

Removing the old keel in one piece so its shape could be duplicated became the first challenge. After unbolting and removing the lead ballast keel, the rudder, the centerboard trunk, the mast-step, and the external deadwood, boatbuilder Bob

Williams unbolted the keel timber, sawed away the other fastenings he couldn't otherwise remove, and dropped away the damaged keel timber itself. To gain access to the backbone area, Williams also removed both garboards and a broadstrake — very carefully, so they could be reused. *Maribee*'s frames and floor timbers were judged to be all right, as were the copper rivets connecting them.

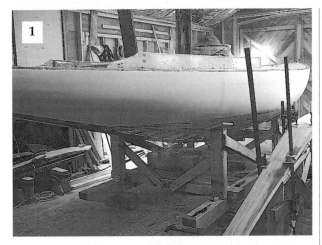

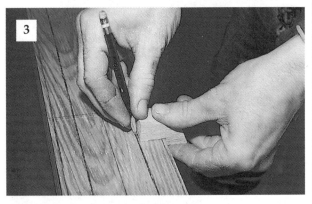

The New Keel

1

A wooden cradle supports *Maribee*'s hull during the early stages of the work and until the new keel is in place. In addition, two shores from the shop's overhead, temporarily screwed to floor timbers in the cockpit abaft the centerboard slot, help prevent the hull from distorting. Here, next to the boat, the new keel has been steam-bent to shape and clamped over a form. It was planed to a uniform 1⅜-inch thickness beforehand and to the correct width as well — narrow where it will join the stem and transom, and about 10 inches wide in the middle where the centerboard trunk will land. The bending form consists of a sawhorse that has been padded and extended to duplicate the old keel's curved shape.

2

This view from the inside, taken just before the old keel was pulled out, shows the 1⅜-inch centerboard slot and the brass straps that connect the frame ends to the keel.

3

Continuous guidelines for cutting the rabbet are marked by running this stepped block of wood and a pencil along the new keel's edges, as Bob Williams is doing here. He'll also mark a line on both edges of the keel about an inch down from the top, to be used in fine-tuning the rabbet after the new keel has been fastened to the hull.

4

Guided by the lines marked on the keel's upper surface in the previous step, Bob begins to saw out the rabbet by cutting a little outside of the line and to a depth that is sufficiently shallow for later finishing with a hand rabbet plane. Notice that this work is done while the bending jig still supports the new keel. (Since there is no curve in the forward and after thirds of the keel, these ends are allowed to overhang the bending form.)

5

A big, heavy, and very sharp slick is used to peel away waste wood; it makes quick work of paring down the roughed-out rabbet.

6

The rough-cutting of the rabbet continues. The tapering keel width shows here at the forward end of the new timber.

7

At the new keel's after end, Bob marks for a cut that will duplicate the old...

8

...and cleans up his saw marks with a scraper, so this surface will land in close contact with the inner face of the transom. The new keel's forward end is similarly cut to marry with the stem, to which it will be bolted.

9

After all the old bolt holes have been cleared of broken-off bolts, and the undersides of the floor timbers have been scraped clean, the new keel is set in place and shored there while new holes are bored through it from above, using the old floor timber bolt holes as guides. Then Bob will move under the boat and run shallow counterbores upward for the heads of the bolts.

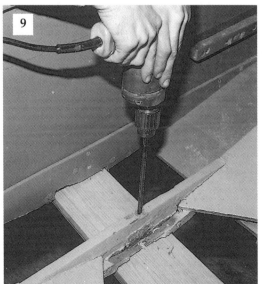

10
New bronze carriage bolts, driven upward, fasten the keel firmly to each floor timber. A ring of caulking cotton under each bolt head will keep out the water.

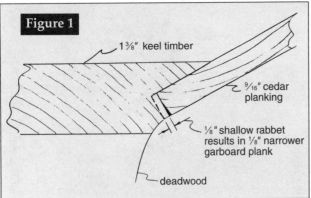

Figure 1 Typical cross section of hull at the garboard, showing how a shallower rabbet allows the garboard's lower edge to be faired and smoothed.

11
After the new keel is permanently attached comes the tedious task of planing the rabbets (using the frame heels and floor timbers as guides) so the garboard planks will lie fairly against them. Because the old garboards will be used, the new keel has been given slightly shallower rabbets, and therefore more exposed width across its underside, than the old one (see Figure 1).

12
Here, the edge of a garboard that will lie against the new keel has been marked with the new and slightly narrower plank widths and is being planed down to those lines.

13

Because, for this repair, the garboard is the "shutter" plank, some cut-and-try fitting is required. Note that the boat's cradle has been removed and that the hull is now supported by a pair of braced posts under the keel and held upright by jackstands.

14

Accurately fitting a shutter plank is a slow and careful process that consists of marking the areas where the plank binds...

15

...then taking off a few shavings, and trying it again until there's a good fit, both along the plank's edges and at each end. Notice that the existing screw holes have been filled with epoxy and microballoons before the plank is driven home for the final time.

16

Since the garboard plank comes to a sharp and delicate point forward, a softwood block helps distribute the taps of the mallet and protect the cedar plank from damage.

The Centerboard Trunk

To allow better access for measuring and clamping, Steve installed the centerboard trunk before replacing the garboards.

17

The 1⅜-inch oak bedlogs will be scribed to fit the curve of the keel's top surface. Virtually all Herreshoff-built sailboats having centerboard trunks also have floor timbers crossing the keel in close proximity — one immediately abaft the trunk, and another immediately forward. As the trunk starts leaking with age, as centerboard trunks invariably do, those two floor timbers, as installed, prevent all-around access. One of the solutions has been to chisel and saw an opening through the interfering floor timber between its pair of keelbolts, as shown in this photograph. That way, the trunk can be caulked from inside the boat, where its endposts penetrate the slot in the keel. (This slot in this new keel has yet to be cut.)

18

Here the matched pair of bedlogs is being planed square and to the scribed line.

19

Part of the information obtained from the old keel is the bevel at the ends of the centerboard slot, made necessary because of the slant of the endposts. Here, the bevel is recorded on a piece of scrap wood so it can be accurately transferred to the new keel.

20

Now it's time for marking and cutting the slot for the centerboard, a task that begins by marking around a thin batten 1⅜ wide, the width of the slot. Notice that the brass straps have been removed from the frame heels for better access.

21

At the slot's extremities, holes are bored — first downward until the threaded point of the boring bit's lead screw just shows underneath...

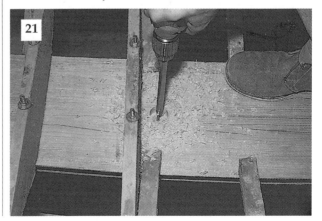

22

...then from the bottom up, using the previous step's small hole as a locator. This eliminates the tear-out that might otherwise surround a bored hole as the bit breaks through.

23

Bob uses a Skilsaw to saw out the slot, running as close to the ends as the boundary floor timbers allow.

24

He finishes the slot by hand, sawing into the 1⅜-inch-diameter bored holes at each end so the waste piece drops out, leaving a slot of the correct width.

25

Bob squares the ends of the slot using a chisel — carefully, so as not to split out the wood beyond the slot.

26

Here is where the bevels, taken earlier from the old keel at the ends of the slot, are put to use.

27

Here we see the completed centerboard trunk with oak endposts, its oak bedlogs bolted to the new keel timber, the cedar trunk sides shiplapped to width, and their lower edges set into grooves in the tops of the bedlogs. All mating surfaces have been bedded in 3M 5200 adhesive. Notice that the frame heels have been repaired with the same epoxy-and-microballoon mixture that was used for the old screw holes in the planking. The brass straps will be reinstalled after the frame heel repair has cured, to serve as the connecting link between the frames and keel in way of the centerboard trunk.

28

With the garboards removed, Bob has good access for clamping and fitting the existing deadwood to the underside of the new keel timber. After achieving a close fit, he will add the lead ballast keel to the sandwich and bolt the entire assembly together with new bronze carriage bolts that run up through existing holes in the lead keel and deadwood, those holes having first been extended upward through the new keel timber.

29

Here, Bob has completed the deadwood and ballast-keel installation, and has rehung the garboard planks. He's using a round-soled plane to shape and fair the lower corner of the new keel timber into the rest of the hull. Notice the low chair mounted on casters, which makes working under the boat more comfortable.

30

At the bow and the stern where there's space to use it, Bob uses his big slick to rough out the keel timber's outside shape. He'll finish with a hand plane.

31

In addition to fairing the new keel, the new oak sternpost also must be shaped so its upper end fairs smoothly into the adjoining hull. Bob does this using the same wood-bodied "backing-out" plane...

32

...plus a scraper whose cutting edge has been filed convex. Notice the newly bored hole for the rudder stock, and the after edge of the sternpost, which has been hollowed for the leading edge of the rudder.

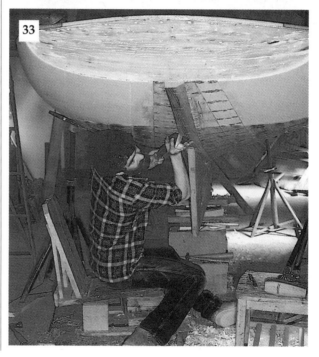

33

Now for shaping and fairing the port side, after which a new oak rudder will be installed. The rudder, along with the new centerboard, will just about complete the structural work.

Did this repair stop the leaking? Indeed it did, according to Steve Ballentine, who still owns *Maribee* some 14 years after these photographs were taken.

Figure 2
Buzzards Bay 15 construction profile, showing how the keel timber joins the rest of the hull and how the centerboard trunk joins the keel timber.

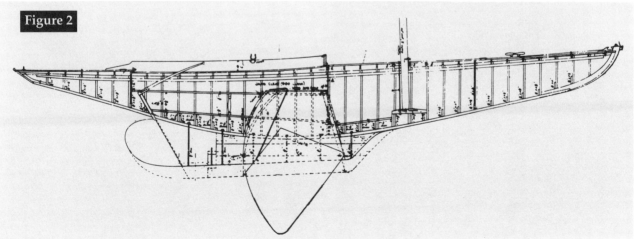

Figure 2